The United States and China in the Twentieth Century

The United States and China
in the Twentieth Century

MICHAEL SCHALLER

New York Oxford
OXFORD UNIVERSITY PRESS
1979

For Sue Gilles, a special friend

Library of Congress Cataloging in Publication Data

Schaller, Michael, 1947-
  The United States and China in the twentieth
century.

  Includes index.
  1.   United States—Foreign relations—China.
2.   China—Foreign relations—United States.
3.   China—History—1900-   I.   Title.
E183.8.C5S3   327.73'051   79-11902
ISBN 0-19-502598-9
ISBN 0-19-502599-7 (pbk)

First published by Oxford University
Press, New York, 1979

First issued as an Oxford University
Press paperback, 1980

Printed in the United States of America

Contents

Introduction

For two hundred years China has intrigued the United States. Though a world away, generations of Americans thought they knew the Chinese well, as special friends—or demonic enemies. Like a magnet over the Pacific horizon, China lured foreign soldiers who plotted conquest, merchants who dreamed of wealth, and missionaries who proselytized for Christian salvation. Until 1949 China lay before them, an empire in decay to be picked apart, exploited, or pitied. When the Communist revolution restored China's independence and power, Americans saw the country as an implacable enemy.

American relations with China have often been confused and contradictory, exhibiting bizarre shifts in policy that reflect drastic differences in national interest and superficial knowledge of each other. Examples of this abound. Americans sent missionaries to save Chinese souls, but participated in the opium trade that ravaged the population. Americans promoted Chinese immigration to the United States when they needed low cost labor to construct the railroads, then barred Oriental immigration because Asians were considered racially inferior. Americans encouraged the establishment of democratic institutions in China, then supported and maintained a dictatorship in power. After denouncing the Chinese Communists as Russian puppets, the

Americans later joined them in opposition to Russian expansion in Asia and elsewhere.

This study examines American relations with China during the nineteenth and twentieth centuries. It emphasizes the years since 1937, when the United States involved itself most deeply in Asian affairs and attempted to shape China's destiny. During the Second World War in particular, American policy towards nationalism and communism in China became fixed in a pattern that ultimately led to bloody conflicts in Korea and Vietnam. Now, almost a decade after President Nixon's startling trip to Peking ended the cold war in Asia, the United States and China continue to forge a new relationship out of a bitter past. I hope this book will aid in an understanding of the immense barriers already overcome and the hurdles that still lie ahead.

I owe a great debt to friends and colleagues who assisted, criticized, and challenged my work, improving it in many ways. My special thanks are due to Professors Leonard Dinnerstein, James Elston, Elizabeth Perry, Ronald Edgerton, Lloyd Gardner and to Sue Gilles. Susan Luebbermann and Joyce Berry helped prepare the illustrations. Mrs. Marilyn Bradian typed the manuscript with her usual good cheer and skill.

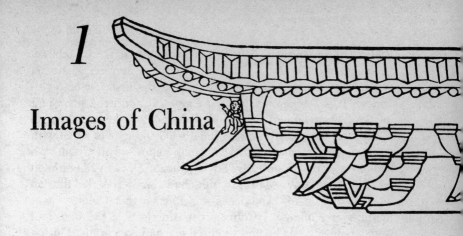

1

Images of China

The news from China on October 1, 1949, troubled and confused Americans. Speaking from the Gate of Heavenly Peace (T'ien An Men) at the center of the old Forbidden City in Peking, Communist leader Mao Tse-tung proclaimed the birth of the People's Republic of China (P.R.C.). During the previous week Mao and other leaders of the Chinese Communist Party (CCP) had addressed a provisional assembly called the "Political Consultative Conference" whose delegates cheered wildly when Mao declared that China would "no longer be a nation subject to insult and humiliation. We have stood up. . . ." Not only were the remnants of Chiang Kai-shek's Nationalist army being driven off the mainland, but foreign missionaries, merchants and soldiers joined the exodus. Mao had already declared that the new China would support the Soviet camp against the "imperialist" United States. Even those Chinese educated in the United States became suspect as agents of "cultural imperialism."

By 1949 almost four years of cold war with the Soviet Union had conditioned most Americans to see radical changes anywhere as part of a global communist conspiracy. Even before Mao formally proclaimed his new regime, the *New York Times* dismissed his followers as a "nauseous force," a "compact little oligarchy dominated by Moscow's nominees." In an official statement in August 1949, Secretary of State Dean Acheson ridiculed the Chinese Communists as mere puppets of Russia whose government could not even pass the first test of legitimacy. "It is," Acheson said, "not Chinese." Former Army Chief of Staff, Secretary of State and Secretary of Defense General George C. Marshall, testifying later, went so far as to agree with a Senator's statement that "what has happened in China is a conquest of that country by Soviet Russia. . . ." In the opinion of *Life* magazine, Mao Tse-tung had "shattered the illusion cherished by many Americans—the illusion that China's Communists are different." China, most Americans concluded, had somehow been lost behind the iron, or bamboo, curtain. During the next twenty-five years American politics would be wracked by the search for those responsible for "the loss of China." This inquisition, accompanied by a purge of many government and academic China experts, helped propel the United States into both the Korean and Vietnam wars.

To understand the turbulence of Chinese-American relations since the Second World War we must look back in time to an earlier era. In 1937, only twelve years before Mao stood on T'ien An Men, another Chinese ruler commanded American headlines. Japan had invaded China and threatened to overrun it completely. *Time* magazine proclaimed Generalissimo and Madame Chiang Kai-shek "Man and Wife of the Year" for their valiant but probably hopeless efforts to resist the Japanese. Japan's armies were portrayed as an avalanche of "ants" driven forward by a primal urge to conquer. The Chinese people, under "one supreme ruler and his remarkable wife," fought for the virtues of western civilization. If he prevailed, *Time* speculated, Chiang might become "Asia's Man of the Century." Similar reports from many of the 1,500 American missionaries in China proclaimed that Chiang and his wife were the "most enlightened, patriotic, and able rulers" in China's 3,000 year history. These praises, when added to the adulation which followed the Chinese-American alliance after Pearl Harbor, help explain why so many Americans saw Chiang's defeat and the Communist victory as such a fearsome event. In less than a decade China had turned from democratic ally to communist enemy—or had it?

The dramatic reversals of 1949 were not nearly so startling

when seen in the perspective of the previous 150 years. From their initial contacts the Americans and Chinese misunderstood one another, reflecting their radically different cultures and histories. Each saw virtue and progress in terms of his own norms and values. What was different was, by definition, inferior.

As an offshoot of western European culture, American social values stressed a belief in individualism, Christianity and representative government. The focus of social activity remained within the nuclear family. The capitalist economic system encouraged private economic initiative in a context of government support and regulation. Technological innovations were quickly accepted, transforming the United States into one of the world's leading urban industrial powers. Despite significant regional and ethnic differences, since the Civil War the nation enjoyed unprecedented prosperity due to the integration of a national market. While inequality persisted, as a nation America soon occupied a virtually unrivaled position of wealth and power.

Traditional China presented a very different picture from modern America. Its culture developed in relative isolation several millennia before the birth of Christ. Tremendous regional variations in geography, climate and spoken language divided the society. Life in China was overwhelmingly rural. Even today, after thirty years of unprecedented industrial growth, about eighty-five percent of the people live as peasant farmers in the countryside. In the United States, perhaps five percent of the population remain on the farm. Although traditional China's agricultural achievements compared very well to those of eighteenth century Europe, the technological and industrial revolutions which transformed the West passed it by. Growing population pressures, the deterioration of government, and foreign assaults, all placed a growing burden on the peasants who tilled their own land or rented tiny plots. Producing enough food to feed themselves and pay the onerous sums demanded in rents and taxes became increasingly difficult. By the early twentieth century, concluded an eminent historian, "poverty, abuse, and early death were the only prospects for nearly half a billion people" in China.

A rigid political hierarchy governed traditional China. Power radiated downward from an hereditary emperor into the many provinces. The "Son of Heaven," as he was known, ruled through a large bureaucracy chosen by competitive examination. While anyone, in theory, might qualify for this civil service and the road it opened to wealth and power, economic realities minimized this freedom. The examination required rigorous training in classical literature and the written Chinese language which involved years of private study. Written Chinese, composed of innumerable combinations, was not an open door for communications and learning. The complexity of the written language kept the vast majority illiterate and only added to their oppression. Culture became a tool of exploitation, a barrier to upward advancement, not an agent of enlightenment.

The requirements of the competitive examination system gave tremendous advantages to the privileged sons of rural landlords, or "gentry," as they are often called, who monopolized most of the official posts. The gentry class were the guardians of culture, law, morality, order and wealth in rural China. Not surprisingly a strong bond of mutual interest developed between government officials in the countryside and the local property owners who were their natural constituency. The gentry often took responsibility for local security, the collection of taxes and rents, and the maintenance and construction of public works. In return, the officials provided government sanction for the economic and social privileges held by the gentry. This alliance assured political stability and economic security for both groups.

Not religion, but a highly elitist social philosophy known as Confucianism, justified this division of society. Above all, Confucianism stressed conformity to established norms and loyalty to one's "natural superiors." This championed a rigid hierarchy of men over women, age over youth, mental labor over manual labor, and gentry over peasant. The emperor sat as head of the whole human family and commanded that obedience to local and central government officers be as complete as that given to one's own father or grandfather. Not surprisingly both the gentry and official bureaucracy enshrined the Confucian classics which sanctioned their own favored position.

The emperor's court and the wealthier classes did subsidize the creation of magnificent buildings and objects of art. But these luxuries, enjoyed by two to three percent of the population, were acquired by squeezing out of the peasantry whatever tiny surplus they produced. Periodically, the continuing exploitation led to local or regional uprisings. Some revolts even succeeded in toppling a reigning dynasty. Reshuffling the ruling class, however, had little effect on the underlying order. Without a change in values inspired by a new set of political ideas, a new ideology, victorious peasant leaders quickly adopted the institutions of their predecessors.

Even foreign conquerors like the Mongols or the Manchus who established the Ch'ing Dynasty (1644–1912) soon accommodated themselves to the existing system and ruled through Confucian-trained officials and the rural gentry. Real change might come about only when socioeconomic conditions among the peasantry became desperate *and* coincided with the appearance of a new political ideology that offered an alternative vision of society. Ironically, the assault of the West, including the United States, set this great transformation in motion and shattered the cycle of one dynasty decaying only to be replaced by a similar institution.

The Western Impact

Before the late 1700s China had very little contact with the West. Arab trading caravans occasionally braved the trackless desert route through inner Asia. In the thirteenth century Marco Polo followed this path and returned to Europe to write about his journey to miraculous "Cathay." By the early 1600s a dedicated group of Jesuit missionaries convinced the Ming emperor to grant them residence in Peking. There they indulged in relatively little religious work but offered the Chinese instruction in Western mathematics, astronomy and weapons manufacture. Back in Rome, Vatican intrigues among rival religious orders turned the Pope against the mission and by the late seventeenth century little remained of the Catholic influence.

China, of course, was not totally isolated. Many of the smaller states of Asia which surrounded it recognized the supremacy of Chinese power and culture. These states were expected periodically to send "tribute missions" to China carrying gifts and pledges of loyalty. The emperor rewarded tributaries with a reciprocal exchange of favors. In reality the system served as a form of trade and political alliance. To acknowledge acceptance of his Chinese host's superior status, the foreign tribute bearer had to perform a ritual—the *K'e-t'ou,* known to us as "kowtow" or "knocking the head"—before a suitable Chinese official. Possessing both predominant power in East Asia and a sense of cultural superiority, the Chinese believed that their country and civilization were truly the center of the world. Their term for China typified this conceit: *Chung-kuo,* or "Middle Kingdom," represented the center of human achievement. By definition, all those outside were barbarians who must embrace Chinese civilization to attain civilized status.

Nearly a century passed between the departure of the Jesuits and the return of a large number of westerners to the China coast. The interval marked a critical lapse of time, for an industrial and commercial revolution had begun to transform Western Europe and British North America. New ships, better weapons and, above all, a new drive to expand foreign trade swept the West. French, Dutch, Spanish, Portuguese and, most significantly, English explorers pushed the frontiers of their empires further into Asia. The lure of China's potential trade inspired countless voyages. Even Colonial Philadelphia enjoyed a small, though lucrative, trade with China. American merchants, almost immediately after winning independence from England, sent a ship there in 1784. Appropriately, it bore the name *Empress of China.*

However poor the mass of China's farmers might have been, there still existed splendid cities and exotic luxury products which attracted western merchants. One early American voyager remarked that China was "the first for greatness, riches and grandeur, of any country ever known." The words were those of Amasa Delano who passed down the family fortune and fascination with China to his grandson, Franklin Delano Roosevelt.

Despite its lucrative potential, western trade with China suffered severe restrictions. The Chinese, clinging to the idea that all foreign contact must be through the tribute system, permitted to only a limited number of foreign merchants seasonal residence at Whampoa, a small village near the port of Canton. There they had to conduct trade with thirteen authorized Chinese merchant groups ("hongs"). The Chinese, quite consciously, sought to limit the foreign impact in all ways. Not only did these restrictions prove inconvenient to the foreign merchants, but the actual economic term of the trade strictly favored China. Westerners purchased expensive luxuries like silk, porcelain, teas and chinaware, while the Chinese bought from them only small amounts of furs, sandlewood, and ginseng, a medicinal herb reputed to be an aphrodisiac. The trade imbalance forced British and American merchants to pay for the bulk of their purchases not in goods but in silver, making trade a serious drain on their national treasuries.

As a consequence, western merchants and their governments hoped to modify both Chinese law and the terms of trade. They hoped to convince the Chinese to establish formal, western-style trade and diplomatic relations. This would ease penetration of the China market and afford foreigners better legal protection. But to the Chinese Empire, such a concept was anathema. By definition foreign states were inferior subordinates who should be grateful for whatever trade concessions had already been made. In no event were the Chinese prepared to exchange ambassadors with the West, an act which would imply equality of status.

The British sent an envoy, Lord McCartney, to China in 1793 in an effort to convince the emperor to sign a commercial treaty. The mission failed when McCartney refused to perform a ritual "kowtow" and the Chinese denied his request for an imperial audience. Chinese officials declared they would go no further than to permit trade to continue around Canton on an informal basis. No formal treaties would be concluded. This uneasy stalemate persisted for another four decades, until the commercial and military power of the West began to undermine and then destroy China's self-imposed isolation.

The growth of an international narcotics trade ultimately forced China out of its relative isolation and into the modern community of nations. Although Chinese had long known of the medicinal qualities of opium produced from the milky white sap of the poppy (morphine and heroin were later developed from

The foreign
enclave near
Canton, c. 1825.
(Metropolitan
Museum of Art,
Rogers Fund,
1941)

the same fluid), it had never been widely used as an intoxicant. Early in the nineteenth century, however, some anonymous entrepreneur discovered a startling demand for the drug within China. Though the origins of the demand remain unexplained, its results are clear. Soon, British merchants began hauling opium from India while Americans carried it from Turkey. It proved to be the one foreign product which enjoyed unparalleled popularity in China.

The opium trade proved especially bountiful for the British who had just gained control over India. The cultivation of opium in India was supervised by the semiofficial East India Company, which processed the raw sap into the drug and auctioned it to private merchants for sale in China. Opium profits provided fully one-seventh of the revenues of British India and helped finance the immense British appetite for Chinese tea. By carrying Turkish opium, enterprising Americans were able to corner a ten percent share of this lucrative market.

By 1839 the trade had grown to incredible proportions. That year 40,000 chests each weighing 133 pounds entered China. Vast sums of silver flowed into the hands of British and American traders. The massive use of opium had devastating economic and social effects on China. But whatever moral qualms the westerners felt, they were mitigated by the staggering fortunes to be made. As one Scottish trader noted in his diary one day, sales were so brisk, there had been "no time to read my bible."

All of this activity defied Chinese law. In 1729 the smoking of opium had been banned and in 1800 additional prohibitions were placed on cultivation and importation. Yet, the weakening and the growing corruption of the Ch'ing Dynasty interfered with any effort to stop the drug traffic. Opium traders connived with corrupt Chinese officials to bring in the drug, while the British government continued to demand that the entire trading system of China be expanded. Nevertheless, the terrible consequences of the trade led the emperor in 1839 to make a final effort to enforce the law. The emperor personally selected a respected official, Lin Tse-hsu, to serve as commissioner of opium suppression in Canton.

Lin startled most Western and Chinese merchants by vigorously moving against the opium trade. He quickly blockaded the foreign warehouses in Canton, forcing the merchants to turn over 20,000 chests of opium which he had burned in a public ceremony. In a letter of explanation addressed to Queen Victoria, Lin sought to explain his actions. Since the importation of opium was illegal in Britain, Lin wrote, "then even less should you let it be passed on to the harm of other countries. . . . Let us ask, where is your conscience?"

Unfortunately for China, England had grown far more concerned with the rule of gold than with the golden rule. The destruction of the British and American opium at Canton provoked a wide assault on China's isolation. The British government, to avenge the great wrong done to its citizens, promptly launched a punitive military expedition. The resulting Opium War (1839–42) not only won compensation for the merchants but demolished many of the legal barriers to trade which China had erected. Britain's aim was to force China to throw itself open to western economic and cultural penetration, to "civilize the Chinese barbarians."

While no American troops took part in the war, leading Americans cheered on the British effort. This pattern persisted for the rest of the century. One of the war's most eloquent champions was former President John Quincy Adams. Despite his stern puritan abhorrence of opium, Adams praised England for fighting a just, if not holy, war. China, he explained, had refused to accept the "Christian precept" of engaging in open commerce. The British cause was righteous because the Chinese refusal to accept western law and trading practices was "an enormous outrage upon the rights of human nature." Hence, the Opium War symbolized a battle between progress and Asian barbarity.

Following three years of sporadic British coastal raids and Chinese military confusion, the war came to a conclusion. The Treaty of Nanking (1842) ushered in a one-hundred-year period of disgrace known to the Chinese as the time of the "unequal treaties," or the "century of dishonor." The previous arrogance was reversed, as the foreign powers now treated China as a barbarous and benighted country. Over the next twenty years, following two more European assaults and an Anglo-French occupation of Peking, an intricate system of law written by foreigners was imposed on a succession of weak Chinese governments.

The system was powerful and durable enough to last until the Second World War.

The Treaty of 1842 gave the British the island of Hong Kong as a colony and compelled China to open five "treaty ports" for trade along the coast. These ports (which eventually numbered around eighty along the coast and rivers) followed a pattern. Each resembled a small European port city, generally on the outskirts of a larger Chinese city. The special zone for foreigners contained warehouses, shops, restaurants and homes. Physical labor on the docks was performed by Chinese workers often directed by a Chinese middleman or "compradore." Inside the foreign settlements churches, clubs, racetracks and parks (complete with signs proclaiming "no Chinese or dogs allowed") were the marks of growing foreign power.

Ironically, the treaty which ended the Opium War made no mention of the drug itself. Britain was content to leave implicit the right to import narcotics. But the omission of opium was one of the few matters left unspecified in this or later treaties. In addition to treaty ports, the western powers imposed a rule known as "extraterritoriality." Simply stated, it meant all foreigners were exempt from Chinese law. If accused of crimes in China, they could only be tried by courts of their own nations. Another component of the unequal treaties was the imposition of a low tariff. China was barred from imposing more than a five percent tax on foreign goods, thus being unable to protect its home market against foreign competition or exclude foreign goods. After 1851 the power to collect even this meager source of revenue was taken away from the Chinese government and placed in the hands of an international agency.

Further elaborations of the system took place between 1860 and 1895, permitting Christian missionaries to travel and proselytize freely. The missionaries, coming from America, France, England and Germany, sought to extend extraterritoriality not only to themselves and church property, but often to their Chinese converts as well. Following Japan's defeat of China in 1895, foreign businesses were permitted to build and own actual factories in China. Thus, by the close of the century, China's independence had been so compromised that it was more a semicolony than an independent nation.

Americans have tended to commend their forefathers for avoiding a direct role in these assaults. While this was technically true before 1900, Americans were hardly innocent bystanders. As early as 1844 President John Tyler sent Caleb Cushing to secure a commercial treaty from China. So soon after its defeat by the British, the Chinese government had little desire to resist western demands. The Treaty of Wanghsia (1844) which Cushing negotiated secured not only the same trading rights which the British had won, but also a promise to automatically grant the United States all future privileges given by China to any other nation. During the next one hundred years, whenever the British, French or Japanese compelled China to grant new demands, the same benefits passed immediately to the Americans. In diplomatic language this procedure was known as "most favored nation status." The Chinese called it "jackal diplomacy."

Not all of China's problems, of course, were caused by the foreign assault of the nineteenth century. A population explosion and the deterioration of the Ch'ing administration was going on independently. But the foreign presence and the unequal treaties added greatly to the burden, and injured China in subtle ways. The privileged status of foreigners undermined Chinese confidence in their own government. The foreigners, moreover, carried radically new religious, political and economic ideas which began to gnaw away at traditional Chinese beliefs. This set the stage for a crisis of culture and self-confidence. Christian missionaries, including a large number of Americans, played an especially large role in this "cultural subversion" of the traditional order.

The Missionary Movement

In our cynical age we too easily stereotype missionaries as either childishly naive do-gooders or intolerant fire-and-brimstone-ranting bible pounders. While many individuals may have fit that mold, the movement was more complex. During the nineteenth century religion played a much larger social and political role than today. Christianity represented not just a spiritual belief but a complex set of values intimately related to the western cultural heritage. Spreading religion, then, meant spreading an entirely new way of life in China.

After 1858 the Chinese government was forced to permit missionaries of all the western nations to spread the gospel into China's interior. Like the gunboats and troops sent to police the treaty ports, the missionaries, both Catholic and Protestant, formed an invading army. Their "enemy" was the "pagan" religion of China, their task to convert 450 million benighted souls. The war budget for this mass campaign came from large and small donations raised each Sunday at church services in the United States and Western Europe.

Most missionaries were dedicated and well-intentioned men and women. They not only sought to convert the heathen, but to build schools, hospitals and orphanages. (Though many Chinese must have questioned why so many hospital beds were occupied by victims of the opium trade!) By its very nature, however, the missionary movement was subversive. Christian beliefs, so unlike traditional Chinese moral thought, demanded that the convert forsake one's ancestors, one's heritage, and even the local system of social and political privilege. Not the traditionally educated gentry, but the minister or priest was held up as the paragon of ethical virtue. Furthermore, many missionaries tried to extend their own extraterritorial privileges to their converts, placing Chinese Christians beyond Chinese law. Not surprisingly, to many Chinese, Christianity seemed like just another symptom of imperialism.

The "threat" of Christianity as a heterodox, foreign ideology was confirmed by the outbreak of the massive Taiping rebellion in central China during the 1850s and 1860s. The leader of this revolt, Hung Hsiu-ch'uan, was a failed Confucian examination candidate who had been influenced by Christian religious tracts. For over a decade Hung and his supporters led a largely peasant army in rebellion against the Ch'ing Dynasty, proclaiming their intention of establishing a new, egalitarian order with Christian overtones. Before the rebellion was suppressed, an estimated twenty million Chinese died and entire regions were laid waste. This rather incredible episode is scarcely mentioned in many western histories, though the much smaller Boxer uprising is prominently featured. Perhaps this is because the victims in the

Taiping rebellion were almost exclusively Chinese while several hundred Westerners died during the Boxer troubles.

The number of missionaries grew continually after the 1860s. By the 1930s about 3,000, half of whom were Americans, worked in China. Despite their tireless efforts, not more than one percent of the Chinese people ever converted. Nevertheless, most Americans had an exaggerated idea of the movement's success. Since the cause was righteous, victory was seen to be inevitable. Also, leading American intellectuals, politicians and church leaders throughout the nineteenth and early twentieth centuries held a deep belief in the virtue and necessity of missionary work. Spreading Christianity meant spreading progress and the "American way of life."

Advancing the cause of civilization served as a powerful motivation to justify the presence of Westerners in foreign lands. John W. Burgess, a leading professor of philosophy in the late nineteenth century expressed the idea this way:

> The larger part of the surface of the globe is inhabited by populations which have not succeeded in establishing civilized states. There is no human right to the status of barbarism. The civilized states have a claim upon them, and that claim is that they shall become civilized.

Crusading groups like the YMCA shared this idea. Its official report of 1895 on missionary activity bore the title "Strategic Points in World Conquest," and discussed the Christian assault on heathenism.

This message was brought before the American public in a variety of ways. Church newspapers, magazines and sermons spoke of it. By the 1920s the new medium of film began to serve religion. Church films entitled *The Cross and the Dragon, The Conquest of Cathay,* and *The Missioner's Cross* portrayed missionary work in China and claimed that all Chinese hungered for the opportunity to become Christians.

The missionary movement inspired a countermissionary movement in China almost from its inception. Isolated acts of violence against church property, missionaries and Chinese Christians were common. Occasionally the violence escalated into large-scale riots. To attack a missionary was one of the few ways an ordinary Chinese could oppose the wider foreign assault on his homeland. Contempt for the religious imperialism of the West was even expressed by powerful Chinese. In 1899, a Chinese government representative told a Philadelphia audience that true "civilization" meant more than using military power to get one's way. "A truly civilized nation should respect the rights of other societies, and refrain from stealing other men's property, or imposing upon others unwelcome beliefs."

But like Commissioner Lin's letter to Queen Victoria about opium, this call went unheeded. The missionary movement continued to be a major point of Chinese-American contact and friction right up until the Communist revolution. To many Americans, China's rejection of Christianity and acceptance of communism seemed like the cruelest ingratitude. To most Chinese the departure of the missionaries marked a reassertion of their pride.

The Myth of The China Market

The impulse to "uplift and civilize," to trade in souls, was not the only compulsion felt by Americans toward China. Ideas of lucrative trans-Pacific trade fascinated business and political leaders almost since the Revolutionary War. American merchants participated fully in the opium trade, but thought of other opportunities as well. They hoped, eventually, to sell American agricultural and manufactured products to a vast market of eager Chinese consumers. Bursts of American territorial expansion towards the Pacific Coast in 1819 and 1846 and later in Panama were partly motivated by the idea of speeding passage towards China. Only in the aftermath of the Civil War, however, did Americans fully consider the potential of trade with Asia.

Interestingly enough, by the mid-nineteenth century the lucrative opium trade began to decline in importance. Chinese came to dominate the trade themselves and began to use locally grown opium. The West now turned toward trade in new mira-

cle products: the agricultural and manufactured goods created
by technological innovation. The very phrase "China Market"
conjured up an image of 450 million consumers able to absorb
vast amounts of European and American exports. This idea endured despite economic realities.

The actual facts of the case scarcely warranted such hope.
China was a poor, overwhelmingly rural land peopled by farmers living only marginally above subsistence levels. They lacked
the money and desire to consume western products. No modern
transportation network existed to market imported goods. Outside the very special conditions of the foreign-dominated treaty
ports, there was little opportunity for modern economic development or trade. Chronic instability frightened away most investors. These factors persisted until after the victory of the communist revolution in 1949. Most leading American companies
understood this reality and were reluctant to invest in China.
During most of the nineteenth and twentieth centuries, American trade with China remained at a low level, fluctuating between one and two percent of the total volume of exports. Nevertheless, Americans seemed to believe that the *potential* for a
vast trade existed and that this required that no other nation—
such as Japan, Germany or Russia—be allowed to monopolize
China.

Ideas about the China Market became more vivid whenever
China appeared threatened by outside powers. During the
1930s, for example, as Japan's armies swept forward, popular
books and movies stressed the theme. A bestselling book of the
decade, by Carl Crow, carried the blunt title *400 Million Cus-
tomers*. The 1935 Hollywood film, *Oil For the Lamps of China*,
was a masterpiece of this genre. In a climactic scene an oil company executive tells a group of starry-eyed salesmen:

> The company is sending you out to China to dispel the darkness
> of centuries with the light of a new era. Oil for the lamps of China.
> American oil. Helping to build a great corporation, helping to ex-
> pand the frontier of civilization is a great ideal, gentlemen. But
> you have the youth, the vision and the courage to follow that ideal
> and with the unbounded faith of Galahads going into a strange
> land.

With only a few minor changes, the words might have been those of later presidents as they sent off economic advisers and soldiers to remake Asia in the 1950s and 1960s.

The Chinese in America

Describing the western penetration of China tells only part of the story of Sino-American relations. It says little about how the average people in both societies looked at each other. From Chinese sources we know that most people had only a dim perception of the differences between Americans and Europeans; after all, they arrived together and acted similarly. The epithet of *Ta Pi-tse* (big nose) and *Yang Kwei-tse* (foreign devil) applied to them all. Before 1900 the Chinese government detected nothing especially virtuous in American policy. The United States might not have fought in the Opium War but it certainly was not reluctant to benefit from the spoils.

Direct contacts between Americans and Chinese increased after the American Civil War. Until then, aside from a few merchants, sailors and missionaries, few Americans knew anything at all about China. Most Americans assumed China to be a quaint, somewhat ridiculous society which epitomized backwardness. The great American philosopher, Ralph Waldo Emerson, summarized it this way: "As for China, all she can say at the convocation of nations must be . . . 'I made the tea.'"

The industrial boom which followed the Civil War sucked in not only millions of immigrants from Europe, but many from China as well. In 1868 Secretary of State William Seward included a provision in the new "Burlingame Treaty" with China to permit the importation of contract laborers. (Roughly, this resembled the "bracero" program in the 1950s which allowed farm owners to import seasonal Mexican farmworkers.) The Chinese were expected to be especially good workers because, as a medical book of the era claimed, their poorly developed nervous system made them immune to ordinary pain!

Within two years nearly 100,000 "coolies" (a term derived from the Chinese words for "bitter labor" and considered a slur) were laying tracks for the transcontinental railroad, while others dug for gold and silver in western mining camps. Despite the fact that millions of European workers had come to America to seek a living, the racially different Chinese seemed a threat. White workers, many of them recent arrivals as well, began to complain that "cheap Chinese labor" endangered their jobs. Violent anti-Chinese riots swept the western states (where most Chinese lived) from the late 1860s through the mid-1880s. Attacking the "heathen Chinee" went unpunished, even when twenty-five Chinese were brutally massacred in Wyoming in 1885.

The American writer-humorist Bret Harte captured the plight of the ordinary victim of this racism in an obituary he wrote for "Wan Lee": "Dead my reverend friends, dead. Stoned to death in the streets of San Francisco, in the year of grace 1869 by a mob of half-grown boys and Christian school children." A poignant cartoon by Thomas Nast summed up how Americans saw the "Chinese question" in 1880. Nast sketched a Chinese cowering before a crazed lynch mob. Pinned to him were the labels "slave," "pauper," and "rat-eater." The treatment which Harte and Nast described added a vivid phrase to the American vocabulary: "Not a Chinaman's chance."

By 1882 demands for ending Chinese immigration became so powerful that Congress, in violation of a treaty with China, determined to bar all Chinese. The Chinese Exclusion Act of that year placed Chinese in a unique legal category. Along with imbeciles, paupers and prostitutes, they were refused the right to immigrate or become American citizens. This law, with slight changes, remained in force until 1943. Then, with China an ally against Japan, Congress replaced total exclusion with a token quota: henceforth one hundred five Chinese might enter America each year.

While the most blatant acts of racial violence against the Chinese subsided by the late 1880s, racial prejudice had a much longer life. The willingness of Americans to donate money for missionary work in China was one thing; to accept Chinese as equals at home was quite another. President Theodore Roosevelt spoke for many when he characterized the Chinese as an "immoral, degraded and worthless race." From the turn of the

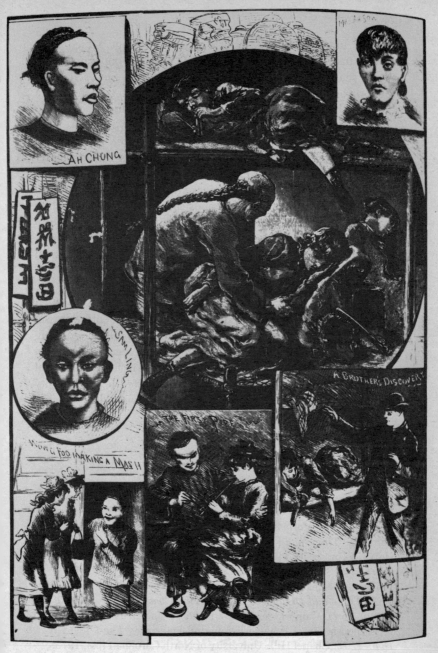

A *Police Gazette* of the 1880s warns of girls lured into opium dens.

century until the Second World War, the image which most
Americans had of China came to them through popular culture
—pulp magazines and comic strips, which were then selling 20
million copies *a month*. Lurid tales of Chinese madmen were a
favorite theme; for example, "Mr. Wu Fang" lusted after the
"blonde maiden Tanya" week after week.

On film the Chinese characters were most often portrayed as
fiends. The arch villian "Dr. Fu Manchu" was a crowd pleaser
and a box office rival to Frankenstein. Fu Manchu personified
that most insidious menace, "Chinese torture." This series had a
simple theme: blood-thirsty orientals conspiring to violate white
women and conquer the world. While some effort was made to
find a Chinese cinema hero (the detective Charlie Chan, for example), what was shown had very little to do with the real
China or real Chinese.

Americans did take pride in their eagerness to educate the
Chinese. After 1900 several American universities established
branches in China and thousands of Chinese students were selected to study in the United States. However, the underlying
presumption of this plan was to make Chinese accept American
values, to become more like Americans. Both in film and in real
life, a "good Chinese" meant one who converted to Christianity
and devoted himself to making over his own culture in the
American image.

Selected Additional Readings

Among the outstanding general histories of Modern China are John
K. Fairbank, Edwin O. Reischauer and Albert Craig, *East Asia, Tra-
dition and Transformation,* Boston: Houghton Mifflin, 1973; John K.
Fairbank, *The United States and China* 3d ed., Cambridge, Mass.:
Harvard University Press, 1971; O. Edmund Clubb, *Twentieth Cen-
tury China*, 3d ed., New York: Columbia University Press, 1978.

The events leading to the Opium War are detailed in John K. Fairbank, *Trade and Diplomacy on the China Coast: The Opening of the
Treaty Ports,* Cambridge, Mass.: Harvard University Press, 1953; a
vivid description of the war is found in Peter Fay, *The Opium War,
1840–1842,* Chapel Hill: University of North Carolina Press, 1975.

For a discussion of American views of Chinese life see Akira Iriye,

Across the Pacific, New York: Harcourt Brace, 1967; public opinion is analyzed in Harold Isaacs, *Scratches on Our Minds: American Images of India and China,* New York: John Day & Co., 1958.

Among the most thoughtful discussions of the missionary movement are John K. Fairbank, ed., *The Missionary Enterprise in China and America,* Cambridge: Harvard University Press, 1974; Paul Varg, *Missionaries, Chinese and Diplomats: The American Protestant Missionary Movement in China, 1890–1952,* Princeton, N.J.: Princeton University Press, 1958.

The treatment of Chinese in the United States is discussed in Stuart Miller, *The Unwelcome Immigrant: American Images of the Chinese, 1785–1882,* Berkeley: University of California Press, 1969; Robert McClellan, *The Heathen Chinee: A Study of American Attitudes Towards China 1890–1905,* Columbus: Ohio State University Press, 1971.

Two books which vividly describe the internal crisis of nineteenth century China are Mary C. Wright, *The Last Stand of Chinese Conservatism: The T'ung-chih Restoration, 1862–1874,* Stanford, Calif.: Stanford University Press, 1957; Philip Kuhn, *Rebellion and its Enemies in Late Imperial China,* Cambridge, Mass.: Harvard University Press, 1974.

A useful interpretation of post-civil war American expansion in Asia and elsewhere is found in David Healy, *U.S. Expansionism: The Imperialist Urge in the 1890s,* Madison: University of Wisconsin Press, 1970.

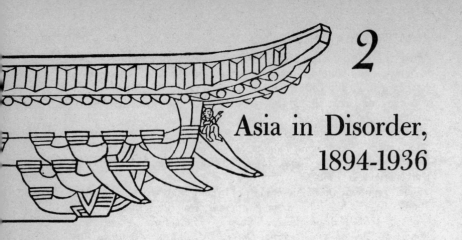

2
Asia in Disorder, 1894-1936

During the century between the Opium War and the outbreak of World War II, few societies had more dissimilar experiences than did the United States and China. For America it was a time of almost uninterrupted expansion—both territorial and economic—climaxing at the summit of world power. China continued its slide into poverty, rebellion and neo-colonialism. The ever weaker Ch'ing Dynasty survived only by sufferance of the Great Powers, which extracted concessions from the Ch'ing court and in return let the monarchy administer internal affairs. American merchants and missionaries, who enjoyed the full benefit of the unequal treaties imposed on China, passed through the door forced open by others. The United States government hardly bothered about China, so long as neither the Chinese nor other nations discriminated against Americans or interfered with their activities.

Until the very end of the nineteenth century the U.S. deferred to Great Britain, allowing England to oversee western access to China. Americans concentrated their own effort on exploring other parts of the Pacific. As early as the 1840s American planters and missionaries dominated Hawaii. Later in the century the U.S. acquired several small Pacific islands, including Wake, Midway and parts of Samoa. The most daring episode of expansion must have been the naval expedition to Japan in 1853–54 led by Commodore Matthew Perry. Under orders from Washington, the blustery naval officer compelled the feudal Tokugawa regime to open trade with America. As a writer in the *Presbyterian Review* observed: "Christian civilization and commerce has closed upon the Japanese Empire on both sides."

Many Westerners expected—and many Japanese feared—that the island nation's fate would resemble China's after the Opium War. Yet due to a variety of factors Japan was spared the agony of internal decay and gradual reduction of the status of semi-colony. Western economic and military powers never dominated Japan, allowing it an opportunity to mobilize its power far more quickly and effectively than had China. Highly disciplined and adventurous Japanese political and economic reformers enjoyed some time in which to reorganize their society without foreign control. By the 1860s a fundamental political change occurred in Japan, marked by the reemergence of a powerful central government which ruled under the aegis of an emperor revered as a god.

In contrast to the tradition-bound Chinese elite, Japanese leaders set about to study and transplant Western technology in order to speed the modernization of Japan. They fully understood China's mistake in rejecting the material accomplishments of the West in hopes that Confucian values could somehow resist the force of gunboats, steam power and artillery. By the 1890s Japan had successfully transformed itself into a regional power with a strong industrial and military base. Not surprisingly this power would soon collide with that of China and the Western nations.

The Collapse of the Old Order

At the close of the nineteenth century the old balance of forces which had preserved a crude order in East Asia began to strain and then break. Inside China nationalist sentiment, outrage over how the existing rulers and foreign powers had exploited China, threatened the implicit alliance between the Ch'ing Dynasty and the Western nations. At the same time, the industrialized

nations of the West and Japan began to compete among themselves for greater economic, political and cultural influence over
the less-developed areas of the world. For the newly powerful
nations, such as Japan, Czarist Russia and Imperial Germany,
acquiring more colonies seemed a necessity to catch up to the
established powers (Britain and France). Expansionist sentiment grew among American opinion leaders as well, though
many Americans thought more in terms of an "informal empire," one of markets for American goods and the expansion of
American cultural influence.

Japan's unexpectedly easy victory in the Sino-Japanese War
(1894–95, fought for control of Korea) precipitated a race for
power in East Asia. A new player had entered the list of great
powers and demonstrated the woeful shortcomings of half-
hearted Chinese efforts at political and military reform during
the 1870s and 1880s. In the decade following China's defeat, the
European powers and Japan began to divide China's railroads,
mines and ports among themselves. The United States, suffering
the effects of a severe economic depression in the mid-1890s, began to fear the consequences of being permanently frozen out
of China through the creation of such exclusive "spheres of influence."

During the early 1890s interest in playing a more active role
in Asia had begun to build. For example, certain American
planters and officials in Hawaii conspired to topple the native
regime and formally annex the islands, despite opposition from
President Grover Cleveland. (Annexation was not accomplished
until the end of the decade.) The American navy grew significantly during the 1890s, a prerequisite for establishing influence
abroad. In 1898 a group of leading exporters founded the American Asiatic Association, which was designed to lobby for government action on behalf of commercial interests in China.
Though no coordinated policy yet existed, a broad concern with
East Asia had developed among policy planners and business
leaders. The outbreak of the Spanish–American War in April
1898 thrust the United States more directly towards China than
anyone had imagined.

The immediate origins of the conflict lay in Washington's
demands that Spain grant some form of independence to its re-

"The Miracle Teapot." A Russian cartoon depicting the "Yellow Peril" and foreign troops in China, c. 1901. (Susan Luebbermann, Arizona Historical Society)

bellious Cuban colony. Once war broke out, the United States moved against Spanish forces in widely scattered outposts. The campaign to free Cuba, ironically, began with an order for Admiral Dewey's Pacific squadron to attack the Spanish fleet near Manila, ostensibly to prevent it from sailing to Cuba. Dewey easily defeated his enemy and in the process acquired control of the Philippines. By this act the United States had taken the first step towards becoming a major power in Asia.

Soon after Dewey's victory, the brief war with Spain ended and Washington faced the choice of what to do with the Philippines. Under pressure to demonstrate his concern over the American position in Asia, President William McKinley announced his determination to annex the entire island chain. In the President's words, colonization would be both good business and high morality. America's duty to the Filipinos, he declared, was to "uplift and civilize and Christianize them, and by God's grace do the very best we could by them as our fellow men for whom Christ also died."

When the Senate approved annexation in February 1899, the poor "benighted" Filipinos rose in revolt against their "liberators" who had suggested they would be granted independence. It required 70,000 American troops and almost four years of bitter jungle fighting to suppress the guerrillas led by Emilio Aguinaldo. Most Americans, however, assumed that the bulk of the natives clamored for the civilizing influence of foreign rule. A typical mixture of metaphors appeared in an 1899 full-page advertisement by the Pears Soap Company. It featured a likeness of Admiral Dewey washing his hands with the company's soap, surrounded by scenes of missionaries handing bars of soap to naked savages. The caption read:

> The first step towards lightening the White Man's Burden is through teaching the virtues of cleanliness. Pears Soap is a potent factor in brightening the dark corners of the earth as civilization advances, while amongst the cultured of all nations it holds the highest place—it is the ideal toilet soap.

Despite the decision to annex the Philippines and establish a chain of naval stations across the Pacific, only a handful of Americans embraced the idea of large-scale territorial conquest.

Acquiring strategically situated islands or land areas such as Hawaii, the Philippines, Guam and, eventually, the Panama Canal Zone was one thing; taking responsibility for a vast population and land mass was quite another. Neither political nor business leaders believed that the U.S. ought to directly acquire part of China or fight on behalf of its independence. However, between 1899 and 1901 these policymakers did devise a flexible formula which sought to preserve a measure of independence for China while preserving America's commercial stake in its future.

As Germany, Japan and Russia stepped up demands on the Chinese government to grant them special "spheres of influence" (sometimes ports, occasionally entire provinces), American businessmen with a stake in China, and foreign policy experts in Washington, feared that the resulting partition would eventually result in the exclusion of all American trade and influence in China. Secretary of State John Hay, guided by advisors William Rockhill and Alfred Hippisley, sent notes to all the Great Powers asking that they promise to preserve commercial equality for all nations in any spheres over which they might gain control. Despite the evasive replies he received, Hay declared that the Powers had accepted his request. These "Open Door Notes" of September 1899 sought primarily to protect the market for American trade, *not* China's sovereignty. The latter was only a secondary consideration for Hay, who never bothered to consult the Chinese government about his policy.

The rather glib and ambiguous American initiative to prevent the economic partition of China nearly fell apart in 1900 as a mass antiforeign uprising swept parts of China. The Boxer Rebellion was partly a "grass roots" antiforeign, anti-Christian movement and partly an attempt by the Empress Dowager Tz'u Hsi to attack the foreign position in China while winning popular support. The Boxers, a "secret society," took the lead in sponsoring assaults on missionaries, diplomats and merchants. In their appeal for public support—and probably to fortify their own resolve—the colorful Boxers claimed that magic oaths and potions made them immune from bullets and other modern weapons. This claim of invulnerability carried a deeper and more desperate message than many people understood. In their agony and wrath over China's fate these primitive patriots turned to superstition as their only weapon against western military might.

In June 1900, after killing the German Minister, the Boxers laid siege to the foreign compound in Peking. Realizing that this attack was doomed, many Chinese government officials and the regular army refused to assist the poorly armed Boxers. After two months of sporadic fighting, an international army, including American Marines from the Philippines, fought its way from the port of Tientsin overland to Peking. En route the rescuers devastated the countryside, looting and killing in revenge for the Boxer's actions. The German Kaiser had applauded this policy, telling his troops that he wanted the Chinese to tremble "for the next thousand years" whenever they heard German spoken. Though few Westerners shared the Kaiser's blood lust, the fanatic rampage of the Boxers rekindled images of the "yellow peril" and "Chinese hordes."

In September 1901, after suppressing the uprising, the foreign powers imposed a harsh settlement which required China to pay huge cash indemnities and permit the stationing of increased numbers of foreign troops on her soil. In July 1900, anticipating these actions, Secretary of State Hay had dispatched a second set of Open Door Notes to the European powers and Japan urging them not to utilize the Boxer troubles as a pretext to carve up China into formal colonies. Yet again, it was not American policy which saved the dynasty and China's nominal independence, but the fact that the foreign powers remained too jealous of each other to agree on any division of the potential spoils. Nor was the United States quite so selfless as might be imagined. Secretary Hay actually approved contingency plans to seize Chinese territory if the Ch'ing Dynasty fell and the other imperialists began, in Hay's words, "to slice the watermelon." In the end, the Powers again chose to permit the dynasty to resume its feeble rule in Peking. It was the path of least resistance.

The Open Door Notes signalled no clear or consistent U.S. policy toward China. Though Hay's initiative marked an expression of American interest in the preservation of some sort of Chinese independence, neither he nor his many successors clarified that interest. China would, it was hoped, be kept open to American cultural and economic penetration. But it was not

"A Fair Field and No Favor." Uncle Sam protects the Open Door for trade against the European powers. (*Harper's Weekly*, 1899)

deemed a vital area for U.S. security right down to the late 1930s. Few Americans, including those most knowledgeable about East Asia, could decide what the U.S. ought to do in or for China, nor was there any agreement about the value of China as compared to its great rival, Japan. Policies during the early twentieth century continually flip-flopped, depending largely on the idiosyncratic mix of interests, personalities and prejudices dominant at a given time. While paying regular lip service to the Open Door, most Americans continued to see China as an abstraction. It became "real" only when threatened by Russian or Japanese expansion that might seal off China or use it as a base for further imperial conquest in Asia.

Early in 1904 Czarist Russia and Imperial Japan collided in northeast China. Both nations coveted control of the resources of Manchuria and believed this area was pivotal for their future power in northeast Asia. During the Russo–Japanese War, President Theodore Roosevelt encouraged American bankers to loan badly needed funds to the government of Japan. Roosevelt feared Russian expansion more than possible Japanese designs. He believed that America's interest lay in avoiding conflict with Japan. By blocking Russian expansion, he told his son, Japan was playing "our game in Asia." Roosevelt had an especially low regard for the Chinese, as shown by his use of the epithet "chink" to describe people he disliked.

Roosevelt's strategic realism towards East Asian relations was reversed by his successors. Fearful that Tokyo would achieve an economic stranglehold on Manchuria—seen by many as one of the world's great commercial frontiers—President William H. Taft sought to restrain Japan. Taft and his Secretary of State, Philander C. Knox, believed that "today diplomacy works for trade," thus leading to the phrase "dollar diplomacy." Influenced by junior diplomats who overvalued the economic importance of Manchuria to the U.S., Taft and Knox tried in 1911 and 1912 to stimulate major private American investments in China. American-owned railroads in Manchuria, for example, would not only be profitable but would enhance the influence Washington could exercise on China, Japan and Russia.

This plan, which also sought to internationalize Russian and Japanese railway lines in Manchuria, failed for a number of reasons. Russia and Japan, though often rivals, combined to resist American pressure and scared the Chinese away from cooperating with Knox's schemes. Taft's view that "A Jap is first of all a Jap and would be glad to aggrandize himself at the expense of anybody" typified the bluntness with which the administration approached Asian problems. Nor were most American investors very eager to sink funds into a disputed region of questionable value with no promise of firm government protection.

Taft, like many of his successors, misplayed his hand by overestimating the economic significance of China to the U.S. In fact, Europe and Japan itself remained much more important as U.S. trading partners. But to Japan, China was a region of vital economic value and strategic concern, a fact which made it very difficult for the U.S. to influence Tokyo's behavior there. Furthermore, American diplomatic and trade policy was increasingly unable to influence the direction of change within China as events there approached a degree of anarchy defying limited foreign intervention.

As has often proved true, belated reform in a reactionary society inspired revolutionary change. In the aftermath of the Boxer disaster the Ch'ing rulers surprised everyone by initiating a series of major institutional reforms. Instead of turning to the occult and secret societies, Ch'ing administrators sought to upgrade and modernize education by abolishing the Confucian examination system and creating a westernized school system. Woefully inefficient tax codes were revised to stimulate economic growth and partially representative provincial assemblies were created to allow the local elites a small voice in public policy. These acts, the rulers hoped, would both appease domestic critics and improve China's ability to withstand new foreign assaults. But the reforms were a case of too little, too late. The dynasty could no longer count on the mutually jealous foreign powers to sustain its rule. At the same time, more and more politically active Chinese identified the Ch'ing rulers as the source of China's deplorable weakness. While those who favored the overthrow of the dynasty had no unified program or goal, they shared basic ideals of nationalism which would unite China against imperialism. Sun Yat-sen (a Chinese Christian educated in Hawaii) was one of many revolutionaries active in the early twentieth century. He and his followers continually plotted the destruction of the Ch'ing Dynasty and the formation of a republic.

When change finally came in 1911 it followed no revolutionary master plan. Instead, a groundswell of disgust at the monarchy's betrayal of political and economic rights to foreigners combined with a series of popular but uncoordinated military revolts which exposed the weakness and isolation of the Ch'ing Dynasty. Many of the recently formed provincial assemblies declared their autonomy from Peking. Yuan Shih-k'ai, a powerful official and military commander, engineered the peaceful abdication of the Ch'ing emperor in February 1912 and created a republic with himself as president. Over the next four years the new ruler tried to unify the nation by bringing the rebellious provinces back under central control and by winning foreign acceptance.

Yuan's regime received two forms of American support during its short, tumultuous existence. President Woodrow Wilson recognized Yuan's government as legitimate despite many questions about how it assumed and maintained power. At the same time several private American advisers assisted the new Chinese government in an effort to impose national authority. Professor Frank Goodnow, an academic expert on politics, worked closely with Yuan and advised him to abandon the framework of representative government that was established in 1912–13. He reasoned that Chinese needed the symbol and authority of an emperor to remain unified. With Goodnow's encouragement, Yuan Shih-k'ai proclaimed himself emperor in a futile move to win national acceptance by reviving the aura of dynastic power.

The Impact of World War I

China's uneasy passage toward modern nationhood soon foundered on the shoals of World War I, which began in August 1914. With the western powers preoccupied in the European war, Japan resolved to increase its own power in China. Japan easily seized the leasehold which Germany had held in Shantung province and in 1915 presented Yuan's government with the far-reaching "21 Demands." These sought to extract special economic and political privileges which would have transformed much of China into a Japanese protectorate. Though Chinese and American resistance persuaded Tokyo to back down somewhat, the incident foreshadowed greater Japanese interference in China.

Yuan Shih-k'ai's death in June 1916 destroyed the last vestige of national government in China. For the next twelve years (and in many areas until 1949) China had no real central government. Regional militarists, often called "warlords," held sway over provinces with private armies. They continually fought, often forming alliances of convenience to capture the traditional capital at Peking. To finance their struggles the warlords resorted to brutal taxation (sometimes collected thirty years in advance!) and frequently accepted bribes from foreign powers. Amidst this chaos, Chinese control over huge areas like Tibet, Outer Mongolia and Manchuria virtually disappeared. The anarchy of the warlord period was a symptom of a deepening social, political and economic crisis. The old imperial order had gone, but no new system had gained general acceptance. This made China fair game for ruthless exploiters, both foreign and domestic.

Ironically, the efforts of President Wilson to restore order to post-WWI Asia stimulated the birth of modern nationalism and antiimperialism in China. Wilson's idea for a "League of Nations" proposed that all major industrial powers substitute open economic competition and cooperation for war and colonial conflicts. As a method to internationalize the "Open Door," the League would guarantee the industrial nations access to raw materials and markets in less developed countries. Theoretically, the League members would also respect the limited political independence of weaker countries. Wilson believed that in the long run this arrangement would prevent major wars and contribute to the gradual development of poorer countries. It also promised to keep markets and raw materials available to the United States and other industrial nations. Critical to this argument was the belief that the U.S. would prosper by this system as long as the competition for trade remained open and free from artificial restrictions.

Despite his sympathy for many of China's nationalist aspirations, Wilson believed it of even greater importance to convince a reluctant Japan to join the other major powers in the League

of Nations. With some misgivings, Wilson agreed to Tokyo's demand that it retain at least temporary control of China's Shantung province, seized during WWI. The Japanese, outraged at
the West's refusal to endorse the concept of racial equality, insisted on this as a show of good faith. The sacrifice of Shantung
bitterly disappointed thousands of Chinese who had hoped that
the League would be a mechanism to protect their country. On
May 4, 1919, politically active students—many of whom were
prominent in campaigns for cultural as well as political reform—
led large demonstrations in Peking to protest the Japanese-
American deal and the grovelling and the shameful behavior of
the warlord regime.*

The May 4th Movement, as it became known, signalled the
birth of a modern, mass antiimperialism in China. Many of the
best educated and politically conscious Chinese lost faith both
in the United States and in the promises of liberal democracy as
a tool of reform. Increasingly, it seemed, only a radical and authoritarian political movement might succeed in mobilizing
China's masses into a weapon against foreign exploitation. After
1919 Chinese nationalists turned away from the ideals of western liberalism in their search for an ideology. Although they still
sought to use the old strategy of playing the foreigners off
against one another, the emerging generation of leaders saw
mass action as the key to power.

Chinese Nationalism and Great Power
Diplomacy: The 1920s

At the close of WWI both Japanese and American leaders feared
the renewal of tension between their two nations. Temporarily,
at least, neither nation felt a need to respond to the demands of
Chinese nationalists. Since the early twentieth century the U.S.
and Japan had been embroiled in a series of disputes over the

---

* During 1904–05 the U.S. was also the target of Chinese outrage. Pro-
testing against racist immigration restrictions, merchants and students in
Canton organized a brief but effective boycott against the purchase of
American products. Chinese nationalists had begun to turn towards mod-
ern political organization as a weapon, in place of the mysticism of the
Boxers.

cruel mistreatment of Japanese immigrants to the U.S., Japan's expansion in the Pacific, and the future of China. American policymakers hoped to devise a formula that might restrain Japanese expansion in China without provoking Tokyo's hostility or a costly U.S.-Japanese naval armaments race.

Leaders in Tokyo and Washington were swayed by the fact that despite lingering rivalries, the two nations complemented each other in important ways. Japanese-American trade was much larger and more significant than American trade with China, although many continued to believe in the myth of the China market. Taking advantage of the mood provided by this mutually profitable relationship, Secretary of State Charles Evans Hughes sponsored the wide-ranging Washington Conference of 1921–22. At this gathering all the powers with interests in the Pacific, led by the U.S., Great Britain, Japan and France, reached a series of political and military accords. The Five Power Treaty imposed naval limitations on battle fleets, reducing fears of an arms race. Another agreement pledged each nation to respect the others' existing Pacific colonies. By the terms of the Nine Power Treaty, the conferees pledged not to interfere with China's political or territorial integrity. This series of agreements fostered goodwill in the major world capitals, but not in China. Much to the displeasure of the Chinese, almost nothing was done to diminish existing foreign domination or the onerous unequal treaties.* Most politically active Chinese demanded that the foreign powers return what they had stolen since the 1840s. A pledge not to take more only added insult to injury.

Amidst their anger, Chinese nationalists of many shades discovered that revolutionary Russia—itself an international outcast since the Bolshevik Revolution of 1917—was prepared to help them achieve national unity and power. Vladimir Lenin, leader of the Bolshevik movement, had adapted Marxist theory to apply to the circumstances found in preindustrial and semicolonial nations. He proposed that a small group of political activists could organize a mass popular movement in China that

---

* The treaty powers proposed a future meeting to discuss possibly returning to China the right of tariff autonomy.

would unify people under the banner of nationalism. The immediate goal would be to throw out the warlords and the foreign imperialists; a communist revolution would wait for a later stage. Lenin justified this approach in the belief that wars of "national liberation" among colonial and semicolonial peoples would help undermine the strength of the major capitalist nations. In an early gesture designed to impress China, the Communists issued the July 1919 "Karakhan Manifesto" which appeared to renounce all the special treaty and territorial privileges held by the former Czarist government. Even though the Russians neglected to fulfill all their promises, their behavior marked a sharp break from that of other nations toward China. For virtually the first time since 1842 a Western nation had returned something taken earlier. In the succeeding years, Russian influence in China would become a major force.

Agents of the Russian-dominated Communist International (Comintern) travelled to China in the early 1920s and there helped reorganize the nearly moribund Kuomintang Party (KMT) of Sun Yat-sen. Sun, who enjoyed a foothold in Canton, dispatched several of his top assistants, including the young Chiang Kai-shek, to Russia where they received military and political instruction.* The Russian advisors did not expect the KMT to bring communism to China, but this was not important. The role of the KMT would be to mobilize a large cross-section of the Chinese people in a popular struggle against the warlords and the foreign powers. An independent, united and antiimperialist China would indirectly weaken the capitalist nations.

Though assisting the KMT, Comintern agents also sponsored the formation of a small Chinese Communist Party (CCP). While the Communists shared the goal of antiimperialism, their program also called for fundamental social and economic changes within China. Despite these differences, the Russian agents pressed the CCP and KMT to cooperate against the warlords and the foreign powers. For the short run at least, both parties needed the others' skills and, in 1924, formed a "United Front." Certain Communists, such as the young peasant organizer Mao Tse-tung, chafed under advice that would have the

---

* Chiang had earlier studied in Japan.

CCP subordinated to the KMT and that called on the Communists to organize urban, industrial workers. Mao believed the revolution must grow in the countryside. He advocated an alternative strategy based on mobilizing an independent peasant army attracted by a revolutionary land policy, a policy geared to the distinctive conditions in China.

After Sun Yat-sen's death in 1925, Chiang Kai-shek outmaneuvered several rivals to assume leadership of the KMT. Despite his training in Moscow, Chiang emerged as a bitter foe of the Communists and began to limit their role in the United Front. The Russians, who had great hopes for the KMT, ignored this sign and continued to aid Chiang and insist that the CCP do the same. In 1926 the KMT armies and the CCP's political organizers launched the Northern Expedition, a military campaign designed to crush the regional warlords and unify all China. Once Chiang had captured the city of Shanghai—a vital conquest since it gave the KMT access to the port's great wealth —he felt free to jettison his Comintern advisors and CCP allies. In April 1927 Chiang ordered the massacre of thousands of Communists and their sympathizers and ejected the Russians from China. Only a handful of Communists, including Mao, escaped to the countryside. The disastrous advice of the Russians— to remain subservient to the KMT in the United Front, urban-based, and unarmed—became a lesson Mao never forgot.

Chiang Kai-shek's purge of the CCP not only brought him supremacy in the KMT, but eased the fears of wealthy Chinese and foreign governments. Earlier he had been thought of as a "Red general." Now he had proven himself a responsible nationalist—both anticommunist and willing to compromise with the rich and powerful in China and abroad. Foreign governments showed their appreciation of this by granting recognition to Chiang's new "Republic of China" proclaimed in October 1928, with its capital at Nanking. He received additional signs of foreign favor when the treaty powers agreed to modify certain aspects of the hated unequal treaties.

During the turbulent 1920s, and especially during the Northern Expedition, signs of chaos and frequent attacks upon missionaries and foreign property had tempted Japan, Great Britain, and the U.S. to intervene militarily to preserve their version of law and order. While some intervention occurred, especially involving the Japanese, the foreign powers kept a relatively low profile between 1926 and 1928. This policy proved successful. Chiang convinced the foreign powers that any "outrages" which had been committed were the work of the Communists, now driven underground. The new KMT regime promised to restrain Chinese radicals, protect foreigners and work for gradual revision of the unequal treaties. Chiang seemed determined to build his own power by gaining the support of powerful groups within China and financial backing from the industrialized nations. Superficially, at least, China appeared more unified and stable than it had for almost a half century.

The Manchurian Incident

The Great Depression which began in America late in 1929 soon shattered the tenuous order imposed in Asia by the Washington treaties. For China, the consequences proved devastating. As world trade collapsed and credit shriveled, Japanese exports were frozen out of lucrative western markets. China, which had long been a major export market for Japan and, more important, a vital source of raw materials, reemerged as the crucial question in Japanese foreign and economic policy. Since 1929 Chiang Kai-shek's regime had grown increasingly assertive in efforts to push the Japanese and their puppets out of Manchuria —long a virtual Japanese colony. Chiang also expanded his struggle against the remnants of the Chinese Communists who had reorganized in south China. Many Japanese leaders feared that a powerful China, under Chiang's leadership, would threaten both their entrenched position and frustrate any plans to expand economic dominion.

Between 1929 and 1931 various factions in the Japanese government and army (who often bitterly opposed each other's policies) meddled in Manchurian and Chinese politics. They could not agree upon the best course to ensure a "friendly" government in China, or how far they were prepared to go in challenging western privileges. During the previous decade cooperation with the West on questions of trade, China policy, and arms limitations had benefited Japan. Now this Shidehara diplomacy (as it was known in Japan)* seemed an outdated barrier to safeguarding Japan's power and prosperity. By September 1931, as world economic conditions worsened and as the KMT regime sought to assert its control over Manchuria, elements of the Japanese army struck out. Stationed in Manchuria since the early twentieth century, the Japanese Kwantung Army staged an uprising and quickly drove Chinese troops and administrators out of the provinces of northeast China. Following in the wake of its soldier's actions, Japan created the puppet state of "Manchukuo," ruled by a boy emperor descended from the Ch'ing dynasty and controlled by Japan.

Despite some heroic resistance the Chinese forces were no match for the Japanese. Nor could China look toward depression-weakened America or Britain for support. While many Americans regretted Japan's aggression and the violation of several agreements, including the Washington treaties, few proposed that the U.S. intervene. A headline in the influential Hearst press put it simply: "We sympathize. But it is not our concern."

After discussion with President Herbert Hoover, Secretary of State Henry L. Stimson offered the government's formal reaction to the Manchurian Incident, as it came to be known. The Stimson, or Non-Recognition, Doctrine held that America would not recognize the legal existence of Manchukuo or any other territory seized by Japan. That was all. The U.S. would not assist China or impose economic sanctions against the aggressor. Before 1938 most Americans, both in and out of government, saw no reason to do more and risk involvement in a Far Eastern war. They wished China well but felt its government must assume responsibility for its own survival.

America's decision to isolate itself from China's misfortunes was neither totally selfish nor difficult to understand. At the height of the Depression it seemed sheer folly to risk war with Japan. China's confused political situation made it even more difficult for Washington to consider any form of intervention.

---

* Foreign Minister Shidehara favored a moderate policy in China and opposed military intervention.

Not even the small number of Americans who knew something
about China could agree upon its meaning. Looking at the uncertain performance of the fledgling Nationalist regime, some
declared it appeared like a glass half filled; to others it seemed
already half emptied. Between 1931 and 1937 policies adopted
by the Kuomintang would have a crucial bearing on future
events.

To the Sino-Japanese War

The Kuomintang Party, which in essence was the "government"
of the Republic of China, represented a loose alliance of militarists, bureaucrats, landlords and commercial interests. The
revolutionary ideals of its early period (Sun Yat-sen had proclaimed a program which included both democratic principles
and a policy of national land reform to give peasant tillers control over their own livelihood) largely died with its founder.
Even during the mid-1930s, its "golden years," the KMT never
really governed all China. Only in two provinces did it exercise
firm control, with partial control in eight others. Eighteen provinces remained under the rule of semi- or fully-independent
provincial officials and warlords. National politics seldom penetrated down to the local level where traditional elites, such as
landlords and gentry, continued to dominate rural life. Efforts
to make the party a mass vehicle were hollow, for within the
KMT, power was dominated by a tiny group. The "Military
Council," which Chiang headed, became the center of power
and decision making. Eventually, Chiang alone held more than
eighty government posts simultaneously.

Chiang maintained this authority by skillfully manipulating
the many factions within the KMT. This prevented any combination of rivals from becoming strong enough to challenge him.
But it also kept the army and the party too divided to solve any
major problems. For finances, the regime largely depended on
squeezing profits from the cities and the modern economic sec-
tor which it controlled. But these were also the areas most vulnerable to invasion and disruption. China's vast interior, where
ninety percent of the people lived, remained largely unaffected

by laws adopted in the capitol, Nanking. Model reform laws
enacted to reduce rents, taxes and usury were routinely ignored
by provincial officials and landlords. Chiang had little wish or
ability to challenge local vested interests. After all, the KMT
itself was likely to be the final victim of any profound social and
economic change. Thus most political activity consisted of various KMT factions competing to gain influence with Chiang, not
to alter the direction in which he led China.

Chiang's peculiar character had a great impact on the party
he led. Though celebrated as personally incorruptible, this
meant nothing. After all, commented one cynic, "a man who had
everything he could possibly want could afford to be honest."
The real corruption was in the nature of the KMT's policy, and
in the interests it served. Theodore White, a perceptive American journalist who studied Chiang closely, noted that as a politician he "dealt in force rather than ideas."

> Any concept of China that differed from his own was treated with
> as much hostility as any enemy division. In both Party and govern-
> ment, above honest experience or ability, he insisted on the one
> qualification of complete, unconditional loyalty to himself. Since
> loyalty involved agreement, Chiang became a sage.*

What vision did this "sage" have of China's past and future?
In 1943 Chiang published his masterwork. Entitled *China's Destiny*, the study blamed virtually all of China's ills on the impact
of western ideas and imperialism. As a cure Chiang proposed
to blend traditional Confucian ideas and modern fascism. He
seemed unable to conceive of progress in any way other than as
the creation of a garrison state. Chiang's politics ignored the demands of China's peasants for basic justice. The book's violent
antiforeign tone proved such an embarrassment when read by
foreigners that Chinese censors tried to prevent Americans from
obtaining copies.

Chiang's failure to understand the plight of or to assist China's
poor marked his greatest failing. He proved far more successful
in wooing the favor of Americans. Before his purge of the Communists and expulsion of Russian advisors, many foreigners had

---

* White and Jacoby, *Thunder Out of China*, p. 126.

thought of Chiang as a radical, antiforeign nationalist. His sudden shift in 1927 led to a reassessment. When Chiang remarried that same year, the peculiar circumstances of the wedding won the Chinese leader many new friends abroad. In China the Soong family represented a combination of great political and economic power. T. V. Soong was a powerful, American-educated banker. His three sisters also did much to enhance the family. Soong Ching-ling was the widow of Sun Yat-sen. Soong Ai-ling married another important banker, H. H. Kung. Chiang Kai-shek courted the youngest daughter, Soong Mei-ling. Before winning her family's approval, the ambitious political leader consented to divorce his first wife and become a Methodist. In a deft stroke, Chiang linked the fortunes of one of the richest and most influential Chinese families to his own.

The entire foreign community in China, especially the missionaries, were thrilled by the romance and what it signified. The public conversion to Christianity by China's new leader and his marriage to an American-educated woman represented a rapid advance in the long struggle to convert China. Chiang actively cultivated this belief by inviting many missionaries to assist token educational and health programs. Most ostentatious of these was the Chiangs' pet project launched in 1934. The so-called New Life Movement represented a simplistic, even cynical, blend of Confucian dogma and Christian values. It took the place of real social reform. The Movement, complete with missionary advisors, implored Chinese peasants to "correct their posture," avoid spitting on floors, pursue "right conduct," and, most important, respect existing government and social authority. Obedience to party and landlord was the peasant's primary duty. In general, the foreign community and missionaries in China responded enthusiastically to these and similar efforts at KMT "reform."

Unfortunately, moral uplift and conversion were not enough to solve China's internal problems, nor would they deter Japanese imperialism. After a brief hiatus, Japanese pressure against north China resumed in 1936. In that year Tokyo also joined Germany and Italy in forming the Anti-Comintern Pact. Resistance to "communism" began to be heralded as the excuse for Japan to undertake renewed expansion in Asia.

Despite these mounting dangers, Chiang concentrated almost all his attention and strength against his domestic rivals. Between 1931 and 1934 the Nationalist armies launched five massive "Bandit Extermination Campaigns" against the Communist forces who had regrouped under Mao Tse-tung and created a small "Soviet" area in the mountains of Kiangsi province. By 1934 the vastly superior KMT armies were on the verge of overrunning the Communist base when Mao and 100,000 troops broke out of the encirclement. The fleeing Communists began what became known as the "Long March," a year-long retreat over 6,000 miles in length. Only about 30,000 of the original force reached the final destination in remote northwestern Shensi province. The incredible hardships endured during the march, including continual battles, hunger, and disease, became a legend in the chronicles of revolutionary struggle.*

Even after the Long March ended, Chiang continued to pursue the Communists. Late in 1936 he journeyed to the city of Sian to prod his own reluctant commanders into stepping up the offensive. Several KMT generals, including Chang Hsueh-liang in Sian, believed that the internal war against the Communists made China easy prey to Japan. Chang and his supporters pressed Chiang Kai-shek to form a new United Front with the Communists which would rally all Chinese against the foreign aggressor. On December 13, 1936, news reached the outside world that the KMT dissidents at Sian had seized Chiang in order to compel him to form a new United Front. During the next two weeks the fate of China dangled by a thread.

Throughout the crisis, both the United States and the Soviet Union strongly endorsed a settlement which would save Chiang's life and leadership. Most observers believed his death would lead to greater anarchy and almost certain Japanese intervention. President Franklin D. Roosevelt, who had previously shown little interest in assisting China, informed the American ambassador in Nanking, Nelson Johnson, that Chiang's survival

* The first Westerner to publicize this event was the young American journalist, Edgar Snow, who interviewed Mao. Snow's classic account, in *Red Star Over China* (1938), remains a major source of information even today. Almost thirty-five years later, Snow served as middleman in forwarding Mao's invitation to Richard Nixon to visit China.

was of grave concern to "the whole world." The Soviet Union echoed this theme, declaring that only Chiang could unite China against Japan—and thus help keep Japan from threatening Russian territory. Admiral Harry Yarnell, commander of the American Asiatic Fleet, declared Chiang's life to be almost sacred. The KMT leader was a "Man of Destiny" who "personified China." If he were killed Japan might easily sweep all Asia.

The fears expressed inside China and abroad were quieted by the resolution of the kidnapping on Christmas Day. Intensive negotiations between Chiang, his captors and Communist representatives at Sian led to an informal agreement that Chiang be freed and the anticommunist campaign halted. The second United Front which developed after Sian was never well defined, but seemed to promise that China might now deter, or better resist, Japanese aggression. Chiang was widely hailed as a hero, saviour, and "indispensable leader." In the view of many Americans China had ceased to be an abstraction. Chiang Kaishek had become China.

Selected Additional Readings

Three interpretations of American expansion at the turn of the century shed light on U.S. China policy. Walter LeFeber, *The New Empire: An Interpretation of American Expansion, 1860–1898.* Ithaca, N.Y.: Cornell University Press, 1963; Thomas J. McCormick, *China Market: America's Quest for Informal Empire, 1893–1901,* Chicago: Quandrangle Books, 1967; David Healy, *U.S. Expansion: The Imperialist Urge in the 1890s,* Madison: University of Wisconsin Press, 1970.

William Appleman Williams, *The Tragedy of American Diplomacy,* 1st ed., Cleveland: World Publishing Co., 1959, places U.S. Asian policy in an overall ideological context. The specific goals and tactics of the U.S. in China from the late 1890s through 1921 are analyzed in Marilyn Young, *The Rhetoric of Empire: American China Policy, 1895–1901,* Cambridge, Mass.: Harvard University Press, 1968; Michael Hunt, *Frontier Defense and the Open Door: Manchuria in Chinese American Relations, 1895–1911,* New Haven, Conn.: Yale University Press, 1973; Jerry Israel, *Progressivism and the Open Door America and China, 1905–1921,* Pittsburgh: University of Pittsburgh Press, 1971; Paul Varg, *The Making of a Myth: The United States and China, 1879–1912*, East Lansing: Michigan State University Press, 1968.

The growth of modern Chinese nationalism is explained in several excellent studies. Chow Tse-tung, *The May Fourth Movement*, Cambridge, Mass.: Harvard University Press, 1960; Lucien Bianco, *The Origins of the Chinese Revolution, 1915–1949*, Stanford, Calif.: Stanford University Press, 1971.

The origins of U.S.-Japanese tension and attempts by the two nations to find common interests are outlined in Akira Iriye, *Pacific Estrangement: Japanese and American Expansion, 1879–1911*, Cambridge, Mass.: Harvard University Press, 1972; Akira Iriye, *After Imperialism: The Search for a New Order in the Far East, 1921–1931*, Cambridge, Mass.: Harvard University Press, 1965.

The U.S. Government's policy toward China's turmoil during the 1920s is discussed in Dorothy Borg, *American Policy and the Chinese Revolution 1925–1928*, New York: Macmillan Co., 1947.

French novelist Andre Malraux captures the drama of the KMT-CCP split in his classic account, *Man's Fate*, New York: Modern Library, 1934.

For three views of China during the "Nanking Decade" see Edgar Snow, *Red Star Over China*, New York: Random House, 1938; James C. Thomson, *While China Faced West: American Reformers in Nationalist China, 1927–1937*, Cambridge, Mass.: Harvard University Press, 1969; James Sheridan, *China in Disintegration: The Republican Era in Chinese History*, New York: The Free Press, 1975.

American reaction to Japanese aggression during the mid-1930s is studied clearly in Dorothy Borg, *The United States and the Far Eastern Crisis of 1933–1938*, Cambridge, Mass.: Harvard University Press, 1964.

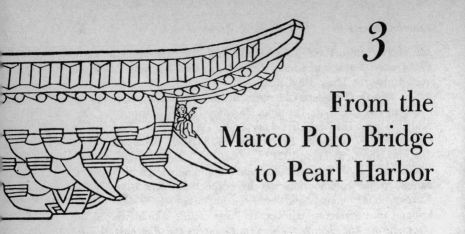

3

From the Marco Polo Bridge to Pearl Harbor

The year 1937 promised great things for China. Chiang Kai-shek had seemingly clutched victory out of the jaws of defeat at Sian. A leading Chinese newspaper prophesied on January 1 that from this day on, "China will have only the United Front, and never again will there be internal hostility." Within China and abroad many influential persons believed that united, the Nationalists and Communists might finally conquer chaos and show a common front to Japan. The optimism lasted a mere six months. Japanese leaders looked with horror at the spectacle of mobilized Chinese patriotism, for it was a major impediment to Tokyo's plan to create an empire stretching across the Pacific. On July 7, 1937, Japanese troops stationed near the Marco Polo Bridge outside Peking provoked an incident with Chinese soldiers that quickly escalated. Tokyo insisted that any settlement grant them greater political control over north China. Patriotic fervor in China made it impossible for Chiang to compromise as he had done in 1931 over Manchuria. Both sides rushed reinforcements to the battle and soon China and Japan were engulfed in a massive undeclared war.

Japan's invasion of China, which seemed to many Americans

a copy of Nazi behavior in Europe, profoundly altered the complacent attitudes of the U.S. After the first year of the Sino-Japanese war, policymakers in Washington began to view Nationalist China as more than a victim of attack. It became a potentially vital ally in an American strategy to contain Japan and construct a new order in Asia. This alliance between the Kuomintang and the United States not only shaped the course of WWII but affected policy in Asia for a quarter century afterwards.

Despite a few early Chinese victories, the Japanese army succeeded in overrunning the major ports, cities and lines of communication along China's coasts and rivers. After about eighteen months Japan controlled all that it deemed important, roughly the eastern third of China. Rather than sacrifice his strength in what appeared a futile campaign, Chiang settled upon a strategy of "trading space for time." The KMT government and armies gradually withdrew southwest, into China's vast interior. From the provisional capital of Chungking (largely inaccessible by river and rail and often shielded from air attack by wretched weather) Chiang would conduct a campaign of attrition, waiting until Japan either overextended its forces or blundered into a war with the Western powers.

Initially, most Americans reacted to this spectacle with a sense of detachment. As with the attack on Manchuria, there was no rush to intervene as China's saviour. Instead, leading citizens and officials pondered how best to avoid involvement in a foreign war. Isolationist sentiment remained strong throughout American society. In October 1937 President Roosevelt broke his own silence during a speech in Chicago that decried the "epidemic of world lawlessness." He told a surprised audience that just as health officials must "quarantine" disease carriers "in order to protect the health of the community against the spread of the disease," America should sponsor some form of international quarantine against aggressor nations spreading the disease of war. But Roosevelt's subsequent statements revealed he had no plan of action, nor would the United States impose trade sanctions against Germany, Italy and Japan. Even in December, when Japanese planes provocatively destroyed the U.S.

Navy gunboat *Panay* (then escorting Standard Oil barges on the Yangtze River), Washington quickly agreed to accept apologies and compensation from Tokyo. Public opinion polls taken a short time later reflected a belief that the most prudent course for all Americans in China to follow was withdrawal.

During 1938, however, President Roosevelt, his advisors, and many influential Americans began to reverse their views about the Sino-Japanese War. By the year's end the idea took hold that the preservation of an "independent" and "pro-American" China was a critical element in protecting America's own security. Increasingly, the United States leadership saw Japan not as a mere regional bully, but as a global menace allied to Nazi Germany and Fascist Italy. The more horrible Japan appeared, the more important China became.

The gruesome human cost of the war in China had a profound effect upon American public opinion. In a world still shocked by modern air warfare, the terror bombing of defenseless Chinese cities and the deliberate pillage, rape and murder by invading Japanese troops seemed especially barbaric. Commentators in American magazines now described the Chinese masses with sympathy. The Japanese, they warned, resembled mad "warrior ants" emerging from a jungle habitat to devour everything in their path. The Japanese were often portrayed as faceless fiends, driven by a "primal urge" to conquer. During the Japanese assault on Shanghai late in 1937, a journalist photographed a severely wounded, abandoned child crying amidst the bombed ruins of a railway station. Among the greatest of war photographs, people still referred to it five years later when they sent donations to "United China Relief." One woman from New Jersey sent $3.00 with a note that "it is from my three daughters and it is for the little guy on the railroad tracks somewhere in China." A few weeks after this picture was published, *Time*'s cover portrayed Generalissimo and Madame Chiang as "Man and Wife of the Year."

Members of the American diplomatic, military and missionary communities in China who witnessed the war and observed numerous attacks upon foreign property shared the outrage. Japan, they felt, had more in mind than merely defeating China's army. Ambassador Nelson Johnson believed the Japanese intended to

A Chinese child amidst the rubble of Japanese-bombed Shanghai, 1937.
(UPI)

"eliminate all western influence among the Chinese." Admiral
Yarnell warned President Roosevelt that the war in China was
really a Japanese challenge to "western civilization." Unless the
United States moved to stop Japan, he declared, the "white race
would have no future in Asia."

These warnings, sent to Washington in growing numbers,
aroused new fear about Japan's long term plans for aggression

in Asia. The Chinese, though in retreat, still tied down a huge
Japanese army. If Chiang surrendered, where might Tokyo send
its troops next? Perhaps to the Philippines, Indochina, Malaya,
Australia, or New Zealand? By mid-1938 this concern was not
idle speculation. Japanese officials now spoke of imposing a
"New Order" in Asia, one that would incorporate the whole region into a Japanese-controlled "Greater East Asia Co-Pros-
perity Sphere." Only China, it appeared, stood as a barrier between Japan and the European-American empires of the Far
East.

The Origins of an Alliance

As early as September 1937, some members of the Roosevelt
Administration expressed the idea that "the peace of the world
is tied up with China's ability to win or prolong its resistance
to Japanese aggression . . . a Japanese victory increases greatly
the chances of a general world war."

For many months this remained a minority view. With time,
however, the dominant opinion in Washington changed. In
Europe the Nazis first annexed Austria, then democratic Czechoslovakia. Japan's behavior and designs in Asia seemed akin to
Germany's. As China's military and economic situation grew increasingly desperate, the prospect of complete Japanese control
over so vast an area became chilling. When Chinese officials
spread rumors that Chiang might surrender, a few key officials
in the Roosevelt Administration sprang into action.

The most influential and active friend of China was Secretary
of the Treasury Henry Morgenthau, Jr. An intimate friend to the
President, Morgenthau hoped to prod Roosevelt to take a more
active stand against both Germany and Japan. Chinese resistance to Japan must continue, he believed, to deter an assault
against the entire Far East. Morgenthau felt that Chiang's army
and government, if financially backed by American economic
aid, could serve as the proxy of the United States in Asia. It
could tie down and ultimately overwhelm Tokyo's legions.

Gradually overcoming opposition from more cautious officials
in the State Department, Morgenthau developed a plan for the

United States to extend a loan, in the form of commercial credits, to the Chinese government for the purchase of vital supplies in the United States. The first proposed credit, of $25 million, was relatively small in size but large in symbolic value. Stanley Hornbeck, a China expert in the State Department, joined Morgenthau in urging Roosevelt to approve the loan. Economic aid, he said, was a first step in America's "diplomatic war plan" against Japan. Both Hornbeck and Morgenthau feared that if Washington extended no aid, Chinese resistance might collapse or Chiang might be driven into the "hands of Russia" and communism for support.

Opposition to the proposed loan came primarily from Secretary of State Cordell Hull who feared it would antagonize Japan while only marginally helping China. Nevertheless, renewed Japanese threats against western influence in Asia and timely rumors of a Chinese surrender (circulated by Chiang himself) convinced Roosevelt to approve the credits in December 1938. The most important aspect of the decision was that the President and his closest advisors had begun to see China as a vital link in American security. They looked upon China as the first line of resistance to Japan and a potential base for future American influence in Asia.

Within China, the American decision had a striking effect on sagging Kuomintang morale. The official KMT press hailed the loan as a new American commitment to Chinese independence. Privately, one of the Chinese negotiators cabled Chiang that the United States had granted a "political loan." America had, he said, "thrown in her lot [with China] and cannot withdraw. . . ." The Chinese believed they had found a creditor who would not let their cause collapse.

Between the loan of December 1938 and the Pearl Harbor attack of December 1941, the United States gradually escalated what Stanley Hornbeck of the State Department called the "diplomatic war plan" against Japan. Additional loans were granted to China and restrictions placed on trade with Japan. Often, economic aid was sent in response to new Japanese threats or rumors of imminent Chinese collapse. In 1939 Roosevelt called for imposition of an informal "moral embargo" on the sale of airplane parts to Japan. In January 1940, when the

1911 commercial treaty with Japan lapsed without renewal, the United States government began to impose a selective blockade on the sale of strategic materials to Japan. First aviation gasoline, then high grades of steel, and in July 1941, petroleum and all other products were placed in the prohibited category.

During the three years before the Pearl Harbor attack, Roosevelt and his aides understood that aid to China and trade embargoes against Japan were dangerous weapons which could easily backfire. Japan, so dependent on strategic imports, might react to the sudden imposition of trade restrictions by widening its war. American policymakers walked a very narrow line aimed at maintaining Chinese resistance and weakening Japan through selective trade embargoes while avoiding a general war and, especially, direct American involvement.

Not surprisingly, in its effort to sustain China, the United States became increasingly involved in Chinese politics. American aid proved vital for Chiang Kai-shek's dual struggle to resist Japan and to remain supreme among his many domestic rivals. To insure both an expanded flow of American support and a monopoly of this aid to his group alone, Chiang promoted the creation of pronationalist lobbying groups in the United States.

In part, Chiang's methods reflected a real need to "sell" China's cause to the Roosevelt Administration. Before 1942, the foreign policymaking apparatus in Washington seemed chaotic. Lines of authority and responsibility were blurred. Roosevelt generally played his advisors off against one another until an acceptable consensus was achieved. Since most military and diplomatic officials agreed that the preservation of European barriers against Nazi Germany outweighed the importance of helping China, the Kuomintang was easily overlooked when it came to the allocation of aid. Accordingly, Chiang saw a need to establish an active arm of his own government in Washington which would work informally to convince American leaders of China's great importance.

In December 1938 Washington approved its first loan to China. Funds were actually granted to a Chinese government "front corporation," the Universal Trading Corporation. In part, this was done to make it appear that the United States was only indirectly subsidizing China, a ploy designed to assuage the

Japanese. Universal Trading (succeeded in 1941 by "China Defense Supplies," or CDS) functioned as the Chinese government's purchasing agent in America, buying vital materials for China with U.S. funds. Its activities, however, were not strictly commercial. Headed by Chiang's brother-in-law, T. V. Soong, Universal Trading and later CDS coordinated a political operation in Washington. Soong continually "dipped" into federal agencies and the White House to hire high-ranking employees. Key bureaucrats, familiar with how the American government functioned and able to exercise much personal influence, became paid agents of Nationalist China. Men like Thomas Corcoran, formerly a White House lawyer, worked for the Chinese but kept up their private affiliations with the President and his friends.

Many of those who joined Soong's effort made fortunes in the lucrative sales to China financed by American credits. More important, they forged a personal link between the Nationalist regime and a wide array of government officials. Over the years, especially after 1945, many allegations surfaced concerning bribes paid to influential Americans by KMT supporters. Many CDS employees whom Soong drafted formed anticommunist, pro-KMT organizations in the U.S. after WWII. Tommy Corcoran and Anna Chennault, for example, played a central role in introducing the Korean secret agent, Tongsun Park, to influential officials in Washington during the early 1970s. Park, like his predecessors, tried to bribe congressmen into supporting the South Korean regime. Commenting on this type of behavior thirty-five years before, Secretary of the Treasury Henry Morgenthau complained how difficult it was to deal with American officials linked to the Chinese. He never knew whether they were working for "Mr. Roosevelt or T. V. Soong, because half the time [they are] on one payroll and the rest of the time . . . on the other."

In addition to establishing these operations in Washington, the Nationalists believed it important to develop special channels of communication between themselves and the White House. Chiang distrusted the regular American diplomatic officials in Washington and Chungking. He doubted (correctly) their sympathies and degree of influence over the President.

Thus, Chiang and the ubiquitous Soong family selected certain Americans in China and Washington to serve as their personal conduits of information. One of the more important of these contacts was James McHugh, American naval attaché in Chungking. The Chiangs knew McHugh vigorously supported them and enjoyed being taken into their confidence. They frequently supplied him with "secret" information which he would pass on to the Navy Department and White House where it would be taken very seriously. Between 1939 and 1942 McHugh obediently sent messages to the President warning, for example, of a Chinese collapse unless more American aid was forthcoming. More often than not, these cries of panic succeeded in prying a bit more money from the President.

Since the Chiang family had little trust in their own government's representatives in Washington—and little trust of each other—they avoided regular communication channels and instead sent their urgent messages to a half-dozen leading Americans. U.S. officials were never certain if they had received the proper communication or precisely to whom they should respond. Because T. V. Soong "coordinated" this system, and since many of the messages came from or through his three influential sisters, the staff of the Treasury Department composed a sarcastic rhyme entitled "Sing a Song of Six Soongs."

Despite this remarkable confusion, American economic aid grew substantially by the end of 1940. Early in 1941, President Roosevelt introduced Lend-Lease legislation to Congress that permitted the President to purchase and deliver military supplies to any nation whose defense he deemed vital to American security. Britain, the Soviet Union and China would benefit immensely from this program. Still, the importance of American economic aid to China before Pearl Harbor cannot be gauged merely by its size which probably did not surpass a few hundred million dollars. While the money was important, the psychological and political commitment it represented to Chiang was of greater significance. It seemed a clear sign that the United States would support him against both the Japanese and his many domestic rivals. Ironically, as Chiang became more certain of American support in 1941, he showed an increasing willingness to tolerate an "armed truce" with the Japanese and resume his long-standing conflict with the Communists. Unavoidably, the American aid program soon became a party to this struggle.

The Collapse of the United Front

Even at its inception in 1937, the United Front represented only a limited and temporary truce. While each party hoped to prevent a Japanese conquest of China, both the Communists and Nationalists planned to fight Japan in a way designed to maximize their own chances to eventually emerge supreme. Chiang pursued a strategy of retreat, minimizing large-scale clashes and hoarding American aid for eventual use against the Communists. This reflected his belief that "the Japanese were a disease of the skin; the Communists a disease of the heart."

The Communists, centered in the remote northwestern city of Yenan after 1937, remained a tiny, armed movement in comparison to the KMT. Their strategy stressed combining a program of nationalism with social and land reform to inspire peasants to take up the Communist banner against the Japanese invaders. Eventually, these armed, mobilized and politically radicalized peasant-soldiers could be used against the KMT. In the view of Communist leader Chou En-lai, the anti-Japanese war would also be the beginning of the end for the Nationalists. More will be said of this later.

Although both Chiang and CCP leader Mao Tse-tung understood each other's long-term strategy, neither wished to precipitate a full-scale civil war before they were assured of Japan's defeat. They preferred to defer a showdown while continuing a limited struggle to expand their own bases at the other's expense. Though a few token United Front representatives were allowed to reside in each other's capital, this represented the limits of political toleration. The KMT secret police, headed by General Tai Li, were especially brutal in their suppression of all dissident political activities. Chiang even assigned a crack army of half a million troops to blockade Yenan in an effort to limit Communist military and political expansion. While the two political parties nominally cooperated against Japan, Chiang labored especially hard to insure that no outside aid reached his "allies."

Before late 1940, Chiang's desire to settle the final score with Yenan was constrained by the fact that the KMT, not the CCP, received substantial military aid from the Soviet Union. Joseph Stalin, Russia's Prime Minister and absolute ruler, shared Roosevelt's belief that the best way to deter Japanese expansion was to keep Tokyo's armies tied down in China. Also, like the Americans, Stalin had more faith in the existing Nationalist regime than in the small, unproved Chinese Communist movement that was not under his personal control. Yet, even though the CCP had only loose ties to Moscow, Chiang was hesitant to risk offending the Soviet Union by attacking Yenan. Stalin, he feared, might respond by ceasing to aid the KMT.

During 1940 two factors removed these restraints. In order to meet the growing German threat in Europe, Stalin was forced to reduce his aid to the Chinese Nationalists. At almost the same time, however, the paltry level of American assistance began to increase. Chiang had told many Americans, including Ambassador Johnson, that he would move more forcefully against the Communists if assured of continued American support. In November 1940 he claimed that he no longer had any great fear of Japan, but he did require American aid to suppress the "defiant Communists." An increase in aid from Washington would permit him to cease "appeas[ing] the Communists."

In fact, Roosevelt and his advisors opposed Chiang's idea of moving against Yenan, especially while Japan occupied much of China. Better, they reasoned, to postpone civil war and attempt a compromise solution in the shortrun. Nevertheless, at this time Roosevelt felt compelled to meet Chiang's demands for increased aid. Japan had recently signed a military alliance with Germany and, in November, Tokyo extended recognition to the puppet regime of Wang Ching-wei as the "true" government of China. Wang, an early KMT leader, enjoyed a substantial following in China, and Washington believed it important to demonstrate its continued support for the Nationalist regime in Chungking. Roosevelt, who pushed for approval of a $100 million loan to China within days of Japan's action, scarcely realized how this demonstration of support would affect Chiang.

In January 1941, only a few weeks after this loan, the KMT armies attacked and destroyed the Communist New 4th Army, then occupying disputed territory along the Yangtze River. The outbreak of large-scale internal warfare not only threatened to demolish the remnants of the United Front, but undermined Roosevelt's idea of China as a bastion against Japan. Since mid-1940, when the Nazi blitzkrieg in Europe had crushed France and Holland, the Japanese had increased their pressure on the colonies of French Indochina and the Dutch East Indies. Tokyo hoped to gain control of these mineral-rich areas, freeing itself from dependence on the purchase of foreign—largely American—metals and petroleum products. If civil war in China freed many of Japan's troops, Southeast Asia would become much more vulnerable. Thus, Washington began its first effort to patch up the United Front in China and compel Chiang to reform his own unpopular regime. This involvement in China's domestic politics continued through the end of the Second World War.

A major difficulty in the effort to preserve China's internal unity was that few Americans knew very much about the Chinese Communists, whose political program and degree of allegiance to Moscow remained unclear to foreign observers. One of the more knowledgeable Americans in China, military attaché Joseph Stilwell (who became the American army commander in China during WWII) thought the Communists were "good organizers" but doubted that communism had any real appeal to China's "individualistic peasants." An adventurous private citizen, journalist Edgar Snow, had broken through the KMT blockade in 1936 to interview Mao and other CCP leaders. His classic account, *Red Star Over China* (1938), portrayed the Communist movement in an extremely favorable light, contrasting it with the corruption and despair prevalent under the KMT. Communist leaders, he noted, professed their independence from Russia and a desire to cooperate with America against Japan.

But Snow's reports (and those of Marine Captain Evans Carlson who travelled into the Communist zone on Roosevelt's behalf in 1938) remained cries in the wilderness. Few "experts" in the State, War or Treasury departments seriously accepted the idea that the Communists had organized a popular peasant army worthy of American support. In addition, the aura of popularity surrounding Chiang Kai-shek made it hard to contemplate extending aid to his rivals or abandoning his regime.

Nevertheless, the outbreak of civil war would have dire consequences vis à vis the United States and Japan. This prompted Roosevelt to seek at least a temporary solution to the crisis. For the long run, the President hoped to steer Chiang's regime in a more democratic direction. A reformed, popular KMT, it was hoped, would undercut the appeal of the Communists. For the moment, however, Washington's need was to discover a formula for increasing aid to Chiang while restraining him from using that aid to start a civil war. Early in 1941, with the prospect that extensive Lend-Lease aid to China might soon begin—and as the United Front crumbled—President Roosevelt dispatched his aide Dr. Lauchlin Currie to Chungking for a sensitive political mission.

Currie, who had played an important part in formulating many New Deal economic reforms, now sought to carve out China as his own special area of expertise under the President. Roosevelt, impressed by his aide's earlier achievement, hoped Currie could quickly "fix" the tangled China policy of 1941. After spending several weeks in February and March, 1941, as Chiang's guest, Currie returned to Washington with recommendations which became the informal basis for Roosevelt's actions over the next three years.

Rather than attacking the Communist "problem" with force, Currie suggested that Chiang follow "Roosevelt's example" of promoting liberal economic and political reforms to undercut the radical opposition. Roosevelt could steer Chiang towards democracy by sending "liberal advisors" to supervise the KMT administration, and by playing up Chiang in the American press through "inspired stories from Washington" which said "nice things about him." Since, according to Currie, Chiang looked upon FDR as the "greatest man in the world," Roosevelt enjoyed a unique leverage to influence the most populous nation on earth.

In his report, Currie laid out for the first time the broad outlines of what became Roosevelt's China policy. The Nationalist regime, he argued, should be treated as a "Great Power." Chiang should be given additional economic and military support and encouraged to reform. America's overall goal should be to encourage a political compromise in China, averting both civil war and a Communist victory. These recommendations served as an agenda during the war, locking official policy into an increasingly rigid mold. Unfortunately, Currie's report grossly underrated the depth of China's social and economic problems while magnifying the popularity and strength of the Nationalist regime. The Kuomintang, however "reformed," was intimately linked to the defense of the status quo in China. Moreover, Chiang was an intensely proud man and a sincere—if misguided—patriot. He would never surrender his power or judgment to foreign "advisors." During 1941, when Roosevelt sent Chiang a group of financial, transport, and political advisors, they and their recommendations were ignored. (Currie, ironically, was accused of being *procommunist* during the McCarthy period and left the United States in the early 1950s.) Finally, Currie ignored the domestic risks of wildly inflating China's and Chiang's importance to America. The Washington-inspired adulation accorded the KMT convinced many Americans that Chiang was, in fact, the undisputed leader of a vital ally. This mistaken belief would have dire consequences as the two allies drifted apart.

Whatever the long term results, Currie's visit and the passage of the Lend-Lease aid program solidified the Chinese-American connection. By the summer of 1941 China had powerful supporters in the White House who promised delivery of sufficient weapons to arm thirty Chinese divisions. Despite many recurring bottlenecks, a substantial military aid program took form in middle to late 1941. The more aid that was sent, the greater the American stake there seemed to be. The greater the stake, the more pressing the need to protect it. The situation became, in the words of one historian, "a silver cord attaching America to the Nationalist government. There is no more entangling alliance than aid to indigent friends." This "silver cord" pulled the KMT and the United States further along the road of joint military operations, which had an important impact on the outbreak of war between Japan and America.

A Secret Air War Plan and Pearl Harbor

Ever since the end of the Second World War both the Soviet Union and United States have used "covert" or secret military tactics against a variety of enemies. (American activity against Cuba and Chile, and Russian policy in Africa are examples.) Most Americans assume that the need for and behavior of the Central Intelligence Agency (CIA, founded in 1947) evolved in response to "communist subversion" after 1945. But, increasingly, historians trace the birth of covert warfare to the period of the early Second World War. In order to strike blows against the Nazis and Japanese even before the United States formally entered the war, the Roosevelt Administration at that time supported a number of covert military operations in Europe and Asia. Among the most elaborate was a plan for "private" American pilots, employed by a Chinese company, to initiate an air war against Japan. The object was threefold: to boost Chinese morale, to weaken Japan, and to deter its leaders from risking a more direct confrontation with the United States.

Advocates of a secret attack plan stressed the likelihood of winning great gains with a small investment. The bulk of American war supplies in 1941 were destined for Britain, but the careful utilization of American fighters and bombers against Japan might more than make up for the lack of substantial aid. Moreover, by attacking Japan "indirectly," under a Chinese flag, the United States would assume no formal responsibility and this would minimize the chances of provoking war before the U.S. could substantially strengthen its own naval, air and land forces in the Pacific.

This strategy was born in the mind of Claire L. Chennault, a retired Army Air Force pilot. After his resignation in 1936, Chennault accepted work in China as a private military advisor to the Chiangs. He was a devoted supporter of the Generalissimo and Madame Chiang, believing the latter to be a "princess." After the outbreak of the Sino-Japanese War in July 1937, the Chinese government hoped to use Chennault to win American support for an ambitious military strategy. Chennault and T. V. Soong were sent back to Washington in the summer of 1940 to lobby for the creation of a secret Chinese-American air force.

In late November 1940, they submitted to Treasury Secretary Morgenthau a plan to create a five-hundred plane force supplied by the United States and flown by "private" Americans working for a Chinese company. This "Special Air Unit" would "attack Japan proper," Soong explained, thus lowering morale and destroying industrial plants. Morgenthau, then the key figure in the administration's China aid program, urged approval of the plan in his discussions with the President and with the State, War and Navy departments. Encouraged by his colleagues' initial response, Morgenthau told Soong that while five hundred planes were not available, "What did he think of the idea of some long-range bombers with the understanding that they were to be used to bomb Tokyo and other Japanese cities?" Both men agreed that such an attack would "change the whole picture in the Far East."

By early December the plan had progressed far enough for Morgenthau to hold discussions with Chennault and Soong about specific targets and weapons. The Treasury Secretary hoped they would use incendiary bombs

> . . . inasmuch as the Japanese cities were all made of just wood and paper. Chennault said that a lot of damage could be done using this method, and that, even if the Chinese lost some of the bombers, it would be well justified.

As Morgenthau and Chennault discussed the terror bombing of Japanese cities, they seemed to give little thought to the likelihood of a Japanese counterattack. (Soong was probably well aware of this possibility—which made the idea even more attractive since it would bring the U.S. into the war.) Nor were they troubled by any moral or ethical qualms about a "sneak attack" on Japanese civilian targets. The Americans hoped the plan would deter future Japanese expansion and relieve pressure on China and southeast Asia. The ends justified the means.

The plan was aborted, however, when Secretary of War Henry Stimson and Army Chief of Staff General George Marshall vigorously opposed it. They did not want to send scarce bombers to China, opposed the idea of setting up military operations outside the "normal" chain of command, and feared the whole scheme would provoke an immediate Japanese counterattack against the United States. The President, responsive to these complaints, urged a compromise solution. Instead of bombers, one hundred fighter planes were slated for shipment to China. Because of their limited range and armament, these could not be used against the Japanese home islands, but only to fight the Japanese in China itself.

Since China lacked personnel to carry out the mission, Chennault worked out a solution with Morgenthau, Currie in the White House, and Navy Secretary Knox. They convinced the President to issue a secret Executive Order permitting American military pilots to resign their commissions and sign contracts with a private company (Central Aircraft Manufacturing Corporation) whose operating funds were provided through Lend-Lease. The pilots, who formed the "American Volunteer Group" (AVG), would then fly the military planes given to the Chinese government as Lend-Lease.

By May 1941, the center of China policymaking had moved from Morgenthau's Treasury Department to the White House which distributed Lend-Lease aid. Currie, who had just returned from a trip to China, worked closely with Soong and Chennault in Washington and became enthusiastic about their air war theories. Currie revived the bombing plan of the previous winter and again urged Roosevelt to accept it. An air war, he claimed, would be of immense value for "our men to acquire actual combat experience." Air attacks on Japan would psychologically bolster the Chinese Nationalists and might deter the militarists in Japan from moving against the European colonies of southeast Asia and the Philippines.

As the Roosevelt Administration pondered Currie's recommendations for the creation of a Sino-American bomber force to be flown by the AVG, the world military situation deteriorated. In June 1941 the Nazis attacked the Soviet Union, further diminishing its ability to restrain the Japanese. Japan was about to occupy southern French Indochina and perhaps the Dutch East Indies which was significant because of its oil supplies. These prospects made the idea of striking a quick, deep blow against Japanese shipping, industry, cities and troop concentrations very appealing.

Late in July 1941, as the Japanese moved into southern Indochina, Roosevelt made two major decisions. On July 26 he publicly announced an embargo on all trade with Japan, leaving Tokyo with only a 12- to 18-month stockpile of oil which was vital for military operations and the economy as a whole. Secondly, in secret, Roosevelt signed a July 23 order which would permit American bombers to be sent to China to be flown by the AVG against Japan. American officials hoped this two-pronged policy of oil embargo and secret attack might compel the Japanese to postpone an advance on the rest of Southeast Asia and might even convince Tokyo to withdraw its forces from China and Indochina.

The secret attacks never occurred, for war broke out in the Pacific before the necessary planes could reach China. Even so, the entire operation set a major precedent for United States military planning, not merely in style but also by creating a core of personnel and an organizational structure which could function on a continuing basis.

Chennault and his pilots did fight in China during the war as part of the 14th Air Force and afterwards resurrected the AVG as Civil Air Transport (CAT). In 1946 CAT received American planes as "war surplus" and flew military missions for the Chinese Nationalists in the Chinese civil war of 1945–49. After 1949 CAT became Air America, another "private airline" which was actually a secret arm of the CIA in the Vietnam War. In 1941, of course, no one foresaw the political and military implications of creating a secret air force. Then it seemed a clever way to strike Japan at little risk or cost to America. In fact, it created yet another deep bond between the Kuomintang and the United States.

By the time Roosevelt approved the bombing proposal and the oil embargo in July 1941, war with Japan had become almost inevitable. American hopes that the limited air attacks might deter Japan were irrational. The Japanese desperately needed access to oil and would not have permitted covert U.S. air attacks on their home islands to go unpunished. (Tokyo had at least some knowledge of Chennault's plans, though we do not know how much.) The American position after July 26 was that trade

in strategic articles could only resume after Japan withdrew
from all its earlier conquests and pledged no further expansion.
Neither side could conceive of accommodating the other. U.S.
policy toward Japan had evolved into a combination of desperation and intransigence.

During the remainder of the year futile negotiations continued in Washington between Secretary of State Hull and
Japanese envoy Admiral Nomura. Even the most moderate proposal offered by Tokyo (that Japan gradually withdraw from
Indochina) included a demand that the U.S. cease aid to China,
permit Japan to impose a peace settlement on Chiang, and
guarantee it oil deliveries from the United States and the Dutch
East Indies. To the American government, Tokyo's position still
seemed to be an attempt to force its domination over the entire
Pacific region. To the Japanese civilian and military leaders,
America was responsible for the continued costly war in China,
sought to deny their nation its just influence in Asia and now
threatened to destroy their military and civilian economy through
the embargo. Neither side had any faith in the intentions or
honor of the other. Though not eager to precipitate a war in
1941, the President and his major advisors did not wish to reach
any settlement with Tokyo that did not include provisions for a
roll back of Japanese forces. The only way Japan might prove
its good faith was to renounce its alliance with Germany, pull its
forces out of China and Indochina and pledge to accept the status quo in the Pacific. This Japan would not do.

In November a handful of American military and civilian
leaders suggested that the U.S. ought to "buy time" to strengthen
British and American forces in the Pacific through a short-term
modus vivendi with Japan. Taking a different approach, Assistant Secretary of the Treasury Harry Dexter White devised a
fanciful plan by which Tokyo might be induced to actually become an American ally against Germany. The U.S. would resume trade with Japan and extend economic aid if Tokyo agreed
to leave China, sell the U.S. most of its military production and
join a coalition against Germany!

These schemes did not more than momentarily sway Roosevelt. Almost as soon as they were voiced, distorted accounts
reached Chiang and his American supporters who reacted in a

panic. The Chinese publicized the fear that any compromise with Japan would cause China's collapse. Chiang warned the American government on November 25 that any softening of the total embargo would be interpreted in Japan as the "sacrifice" of China by the United States: "the morale of the people will collapse . . . the Chinese Army will collapse and the Japanese will be enabled to carry out their plans. . . . Such a loss will not be to China alone. . . ." When numerous American officials such as Treasury Secretary Morgenthau lashed out against a "sellout," Roosevelt dropped the idea of a *modus vivendi*.

On November 26 Secretary Hull told the Japanese negotiators that the final terms for peace demanded Japan's complete withdrawal from China and Indochina and a pledge not to seize any other territory throughout the Pacific. Only then would Washington and its Anglo-Dutch allies resume trade. Neither China nor anything else would be compromised. With their oil running out, and all other avenues blocked to them, the Japanese responded on December 7, 1941, by attacking the American fleet at Pearl Harbor.

By the end of November 1941, the basic policy of the United States in Asia was to resist any further Japanese expansion while simultaneously preventing the collapse of the Nationalist regime in China. The Roosevelt Administration believed that a key element in containing Japan was their program of sustaining and strengthening Chiang. More than just a military calculation, the KMT leader had become a symbol of resistance in Western eyes. Roosevelt had begun to envision the creation of a new order in Asia, based on an alliance between the United States and the Kuomintang. This new order would destroy the threat of future armed aggression and steer postwar Asia along the hazardous course of political development. The implicit alliance forged by 1941 drew the United States into a struggle to control the destiny of Asia, a contest from which it has yet to emerge.

Selected Additional Readings

American policy towards China and Japan during the years before Pearl Harbor is analyzed in the following books. Warren Cohen, *The*

Chinese Connection, New York: Columbia University Press, 1978; Robert J. C. Butow, *Tojo and the Coming of the War,* Princeton, N.J.: Princeton University Press, 1961 and, by the same author, *The John Doe Associates: Backdoor Diplomacy for Peace in 1941,* Stanford, Calif.: Stanford University Press, 1974; Herbert Feis, *The Road to Pearl Harbor: The Coming of the War Between the United States and Japan,* Princeton, N.J.: Princeton University Press, 1950; Irvine Anderson, "The 1941 De Facto Embargo on Oil to Japan: A Bureaucratic Reflex," *Pacific Historical Review,* 44 (May 1975); The U.S. plan to attack Japan is described in Michael Schaller, "American Air Strategy in China, 1939–1941: The Origins of Clandestine Air Warfare," *American Quarterly,* 28 (Spring 1976); Dorothy Borg and Shumpei Okamoto, eds., *Pearl Harbor as History: Japanese-American Relations 1931–1941,* New York: Columbia University Press, 1973.

4

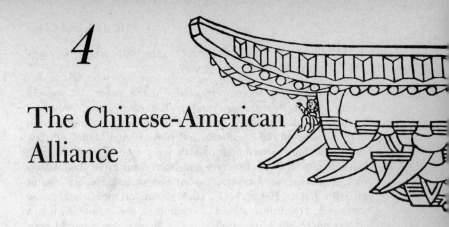

The Chinese-American
Alliance

The startling attack upon the American fleet at Pearl Harbor shattered the illusion that China could be used as a proxy to fight Japan. Now the United States, and its allies, faced the Axis Powers along two global fronts. Stunned by the success of Japanese forces in Hawaii and throughout the Pacific, many Americans found relief in their own nation's alliance with a "battle tested" Chinese army. In an editorial appearing two days after the war began, the *New York Times* optimistically wrote:

> We are partners in a large unity. . . . We have as our ally China, with its inexhaustible manpower—China, from whose patient and untiring and infinitely resourceful people there will now return to us tenfold payment upon such aid as we have given.

Sometime later an army propaganda film entitled *The Battle of China* expressed a similar belief:

> The oldest and the youngest of the world's great nations, together with the British Commonwealth, fight side by side in the struggle that is as old as China herself. The struggle of freedom against slavery, civilization against barbarism, good against evil. . . .

In fact, Chiang and his cohorts privately greeted news of the Japanese attack with unbounded glee. Han Suyin, then married to a KMT officer, chronicled the reaction she witnessed in Chungking to word that the U.S. was at war.

> Almost immediately there were noises in the street . . . people surging out of their houses to buy the newspapers, crowding together . . . the military council was jubilant. Chiang was so happy he sang an old opera aria and played "Ave Maria" all day. The Kuomintang government officials went around congratulating each other, as if a great victory had been won. From their standpoint, it was a great victory. . . . At last, at last America was at war with Japan. Now China's strategic importance would grow even more. American money and equipment would flow in; half a billion dollars, one billion dollars. . . . Now America would *have* to support Chiang, and that meant U.S. dollars into the pockets of the officials, into the pockets of the army commanders, and guns to Hu Tsung-nan for the coming war against Yenan.

As different as these realities were, the importance of the Pacific War transcended the initial understandings of most Americans and Chinese. The Japanese troops who overran the Dutch East Indies, French Indochina, Burma, Malaya, Singapore and the Philippines and threatened India shattered the grip of western colonial power and sounded the death knell to the age of empire in Asia. Throughout the conquered lands, vigorous nationalist movements arose determined to oppose both the new invaders and the return of the former colonial masters. In China the pattern varied only slightly. Japan's invasion swept away the privileged position of the western powers and thoroughly discredited the Kuomintang. From out of the cauldron of the war of resistance, the Chinese Communists emerged carrying a dual banner of nationalism and social revolution, a banner which they carried on to victory.

Until his death in April 1945, President Roosevelt struggled valiantly to forge an American policy accommodating the powerful forces of nationalism unleashed by the war. FDR understood the many ways in which postwar Asia would be transformed. When defeated, Roosevelt predicted, Japan would be stripped of its empire and reduced to an island nation again. Undoubtedly, the Soviet Union would play a more powerful role in northeast Asia. The British, Dutch and French colonial empires, dominant for almost two centuries, would crumble as nationalists seized power. And China, with a quarter of the world's population, would emerge united and regenerated, once again asserting its historical power in East Asia. The great task before America was to devise a policy steering these forces of change in the most friendly direction.

Roosevelt hoped that China and the other emerging states of Asia would be governed by "moderate" nationalists sympathetic to American views of proper political and economic relations. Moderate reform and free enterprise, not revolutionary social upheaval, should be the path of progress. A stable, united, pro-American China could be the lynchpin for all of Asia. Furthermore, China would be useful as a buffer against possible Soviet expansion in northeast Asia. While still fighting Japan, America's policymakers faced the great challenge of creating this new China from the existing chaos. Although military experts soon realized China was not likely to be of much help in winning the war, Roosevelt expressed a vital interest in its future. He told British leaders how China, with its vast population, would be "very useful twenty-five years hence, even though China cannot contribute much military or naval support for the moment." At the very least, China could assist the present war effort by tying down several million Japanese troops. This fact alone seemed to justify extending military and economic aid.

Roosevelt did not divorce China's future from his general scheme of wartime diplomacy. He hoped that the Grand Alliance—the United States, British Commonwealth, Soviet Union and Nationalist China—would emerge from the war as partners determined to construct a lasting peace. There would be, of course, conflicting interests and desires to dominate particular regions. But, Roosevelt believed, they could find common ground in his plans to revitalize world trade, permit gradual decolonization and formulate collective security arrangements. He even felt that America would have sufficient leverage over the British and western European powers to convince them to grant independence to their colonies in an orderly fashion. This would prevent the outbreak of numerous colonial wars and the consequent "radicalization" of nationalist movements. In Asia, China seemed the natural choice to become one of what FDR sometimes called "the Four Policemen" to protect world peace.

Even though the bulk of his attention (as well as American forces and supplies) were absorbed by the war in Europe, for a variety of practical and romantic reasons Roosevelt wanted to include China among the ranks of the Grand Alliance. A circle of like-minded enthusiasts convinced the President he could join American power to the Kuomintang and create an effective wartime and postwar ally. A strong, democratic China would replace the influence of Japan and the European empires, while countering the appeal of revolutionary doctrines among the masses of the East. Another thought expressed during the war by Roosevelt and Harry Hopkins, an advisor, clinched the argument: "In any serious conflict of policy with Russia," Nationalist China "would line up on our side."

Before any of Roosevelt's plans could be realized, however, the United States had first to succeed in breathing new life into the Kuomintang. Without a profound change in the nature of the regime, little could be expected from the "Fourth Policeman," now or later. Unfortunately, FDR never fully realized that in his effort to forge a new order in China he had allied America to a decaying government, one resembling the Austrian "corpse" to which Germany found itself tied in the First World War. After 1941, despite massive infusions of American money ($500,000,000 in gold in 1942 alone) and weapons, the KMT's claim to power and popular support continually diminished. While this occurred, the power of the Communists grew far stronger. Before long the United States became the crutch holding up the losing side in a renewed Chinese civil war.

Warning signals reached Washington even as the fires smoked amidst the rubble at Pearl Harbor. General John Magruder, assigned as an observer in Chungking, warned that Chiang intended to hoard whatever aid America gave him, "largely with the idea of *postwar* military action." Chinese military strategists, he wrote, lived in a "world of make-believe" and Chiang himself looked upon his soldiers and equipment as "static assets to be conserved for assistance in fighting against . . . fellow countrymen for economic and political supremacy." Ambassador Clarence Gauss, a distant, brooding man with long years spent in China, believed that Chiang "suffered from a touch of unreality derived from a somewhat grandiose or 'ivory tower' conception of his and China's role."

These reports were not likely to please President Roosevelt. Like many men, he desired reality to conform to his plan for it. What impressed him most, and what he used to justify his policy, were ideas expressed by Chiang's American supporters such as Lauchlin Currie who again travelled to China on FDR's behalf in 1942. He told the President:

> We have a unique opportunity to exert a profound influence on the development of China and hence Asia. It appears to me to be profoundly in our national interest to give full support to the Generalissimo, both military and diplomatic. I do not think we need to lay down any conditions nor tie any strings to this support. . . . we can rely on him so far as lies within his power to, go in the direction of our wishes in prosecuting a vigorous war policy and creating a modern, democratic and powerful state.

Currie's view of Chiang captured the attention of the President and the American people. Madame Chiang made a triumphant tour of the United States during 1942–43 and the press celebrated China as one of our greatest allies. The Henry Luce publishing empire (*Time, Life*) placed Chiang Kai-shek's portrait on six covers before 1945, more than any other mortal. Who could remain unmoved by Madame Chiang's words before a joint session of Congress? The Kuomintang and the United States, she declared, together fought for a "better world, not just for ourselves alone, but for all mankind."

Few of the increasing numbers of Americans in China after Pearl Harbor shared Madame Chiang's certainty about this "better world." During the war, journalists, diplomats and military officers prepared literally thousands of reports on the actual situation in "free China." Their findings chronicled a regime which perpetrated almost unbelievable cruelty. Tragically, wartime censorship blocked most of the news stories from reaching America; the criticisms leveled by diplomats and soldiers were routinely ignored. Roosevelt and his close advisors were not cruel and insensitive men. But they had outlined a policy which committed the United States to cooperation with the Kuomintang and so became unable or unwilling to alter their course. They became prisoners of their own ignorance and optimism.

The Real War in China

Only by disregarding the inspired news stories from the White House and the *Time* covers of Generalissimo and Madame Chiang could one discover the tragedy of wartime China. Theodore White (later famous for his *Making of the President* series) wrote many of the finest accounts later collected in *Thunder Out of China* (1946). His eyewitness report of the 1942–43 famine in Honan province (censored at the time) speaks for itself.

> The peasants as we saw them were dying. They were dying on the roads, in the mountains, by the railway stations, in their mud huts, in the fields. And as they died, the government continued to wring from them the last possible ounce of tax. . . . The government in county after county was demanding of the peasant more . . . grain than he had raised. . . . No excuses were allowed; peasants who were eating elm bark and dried leaves had to haul their last sack of seed grain to the tax collector's office. Peasants who were so weak they could barely walk had to collect fodder for the army's horses. . . . One of the most macabre touches of all this was the flurry of land speculation. Merchants . . . small government officials, army officials and rich land owners who still had food were engaged in purchasing the peasants' ancestral areas at criminally low figures. . . . we knew that there was a fury, as cold and relentless as death itself, in the bosom of the peasants of Honan, that their loyalty had been hollowed to nothingness by the extortion of their government.

This horror, occurring in many other regions of China during the war, belied Madame Chiang's pious words about the better world for which the KMT fought. Lacking virtually all principles save for anticommunism and a dedication to greed, the Nationalist regime allowed its adherents to indulge in an orgy of selfishness. Nor were its long-term prospects much better. Chiang's dependence on the landlords and rural gentry made it almost impossible for him to answer the peasants' cry for social justice. Yet, only the rosy propaganda about KMT China reached

the American public. American political leaders all too easily
believed the images they helped to create.

American Military Strategy and the KMT

When Chiang requested that President Roosevelt send a military
advisor to Chungking, T. V. Soong (by then the Chinese foreign
minister) had suggested that "the officer need not be an expert
on the Far East." On the contrary, Chiang hoped Washington
would send a "yes-man" whose function it would be to endorse
aid requests. Ironically, the officer selected was General Joseph
W. Stilwell, who knew more about China than practically anyone else in the army. "Vinegar Joe," as he was affectionately
known by his troops, was a tough, no-nonsense soldier who had
spent years in China as a young officer and military attaché.
During the 1920s and 1930s he had learned Chinese and travelled widely in the countryside. A life-long friend of Army Chief
of Staff General George C. Marshall, Stilwell seemed an inspired
choice to serve as commander of U.S. forces in China and advisor to Chiang Kai-shek. Theoretically, he could take charge of
the American aid effort and assist Chiang's armies in organizing
an offensive against Japanese forces in China.

Almost three years later, in the fall of 1944, a despondent
General Stilwell described how political in-fighting had undercut all his efforts in China. "American aid," Stilwell complained,
"had to take into consideration the domestic side of every move
we have undertaken . . . so that that Gimo's [Generalissimo
Chiang] own command will get the most benefit from it." All
serious military initiative had been sacrificed to achieve Roosevelt's goal of "preserving China's precarious unity" under
Chiang's leadership. "The cure for China's trouble is the elimina-
tion of Chiang Kai-shek," concluded Stilwell.

These sombre judgments had begun to form in Stilwell's mind
almost as soon as he reached China in March 1942. Although his
actual authority was unclear, the American general immediately
attempted to assume command of the Chinese forces fighting in
Burma to keep the Burma Road open. This land route was crucial for bringing military supplies into China from India. Chiang,

Generalissimo Chiang Kai-shek and General Stilwell in a lighter moment, 1943. (National Archives)

however, failed to understand why the Americans bothered. Instead, he felt, they could fly supplies into China over the treacherous Himalayan air route known as the "Hump." Though air transportation was costly and dangerous, it did not require that Chiang sacrifice KMT soldiers and weapons in its defense. For the rest of the war, Chiang struggled to avoid using his troops to open a land route into China.

Not surprisingly, the Japanese quickly overran Burma and effectively isolated China in the spring of 1942. The disaster in Burma convinced Stilwell that China could only play an important role in the war if its armies were thoroughly reorganized and used to reopen Burma. This would permit substantial supplies to reach China and allow a still more powerful army to take the field against Japanese forces. For the next two and one-half years Stilwell fought against overwhelming odds to create and command this "new army." "While the wasteful and inefficient system of juggling" of Chinese armies might be necessary to maintain Chiang's power, he wrote, "it emasculated the effectiveness of Chinese troops." But even Stilwell failed to fully realize that his plans for drastic military reform threatened to topple the whole jerrybuilt structure of Nationalist power.

As of 1942 the Chinese army, if it could even be called an army in the modern sense, consisted of about 3,800,000 men in 316 divisions. Only about 30 divisions were considered personally loyal to Chiang. The rest were divided among twelve zonal commanders who were tied to Chiang in a loose coalition. The quality of most of these troops (except for the crack army of 400,000 commanded by Hu Tsung-nan which surrounded the Communist capital of Yenan) can be gauged by a report prepared by American army officials in 1945. The report chronicled the formation of a typical Chinese unit.

> Conscription: Conscription comes to the Chinese peasant like famine or flood, only more regularly—every year twice—and claims more victims. Famine, flood, and drought compare with conscription like chicken pox with plague.
>
> The virus is spread over the Chinese countryside. . . . There is first the press gang. For example you are working in the field looking after your rice . . . [there come] a number of men who tie your hands behind your back and take you with them. . . . Hoe and plow rust in the field, the wife runs to the magistrate to cry and beg for her husband, the children starve.

The report then described how prison officials made money by selling convicts into army service. Together all the conscripts

A group of Chiang Kai-shek's top officers. (National Archives)

were marched hundreds of miles to training camps. Those who could fled along the way. Those caught were beaten and forced to march on. Disease took an increasingly heavy toll. Soon the true "value" of the new conscripts emerged. Officers could "pocket a conscript's pay and his rations can be sold. That makes him a valuable member of the Chinese Army and that is the basis of the demand for him."

If somebody dies, his body is left behind. His name on the list is carried along. As long as his death is not reported, he continues to be a source of income, increased by the fact he has ceased to consume. His rice and his pay become a long-lasting token of memory in the pocket of his commanding officer. His family will have to forget him.

Reading this official report (which also compared Chinese army hospitals to Nazi concentration camps) the description seemed as if it were meant to condemn the Germans and Japanese rather than America's ally.

No American was more horrified by these conditions than General Stilwell. He quickly developed a policy aimed at reforming the Chinese army by reducing its overall size and selecting thirty divisions for special training. These new divisions, commanded by a Chinese officer chosen by Stilwell, would lead the proposed Burma campaign and form the nucleus of a powerful military force in China.

What Stilwell never sufficiently accounted for was that his plan to restructure the Chinese army and distribute American arms to selected divisions led by hand-picked commanders involved many more political than military questions. In his diary Stilwell wrote, "Why doesn't the little dummy [Chiang] realize that his only hope is the 30 division plan, and the creation of a separate, efficient, well equipped and well trained force?" But Chiang, in his own way, did fully understand what Stilwell's reforms envisioned. They would cut out the heart of Chiang's power structure. No longer would he alone be able to control the contentious KMT factions through selecting commanders and distributing aid to those personally loyal. Instead, the Americans, and *their* Chinese commanders, would become the masters of China's KMT armies. Chiang would become extraneous and expendable. Understandably the Generalissimo did everything possible to prevent this, by delaying approval of Stilwell's plans and trying to convince Roosevelt to recall the troublesome American.

Stilwell grew increasingly infuriated by Chiang's refusal to initiate a Burma campaign or support the army reform program. "The stupid little ass fails to grasp the opportunity of his life," Stilwell complained. "The Chinese government," he concluded, was "a structure based on fear and favor, in the hands of an ignorant and stubborn man. . . ." Dismissing Chiang with the epithet "Peanut," Stillwell concluded: "Only outside influence can do anything for China—either enemy action will smash her or some regenerative idea must be formed and put into effect at once." By the end of 1942, Stilwell believed he himself embodied that regenerative idea and he began to compete with Chiang for control of China's armies. The weapon Stilwell sought was Roosevelt's support in the form of an order to Chiang: let the American general distribute aid as he saw fit and lead all Chinese forces in combat. In short, let Stilwell act as commander of China. Such an order did not come until September 1944, and was countermanded almost as quickly as it appeared.

From late 1942 until the summer of 1944 Chiang successfully resisted Stilwell. The Generalissimo understood that Roosevelt hoped to utilize China as an American protégé in Asia, a stabilizing influence to take the place of Japan and the European colonial empires and to provide a counterweight to Soviet influence. In the long run, Chiang believed, FDR would not act to alienate or undercut the Nationalist regime which he championed as one of the future "Four Policemen."

The Chinese Manipulation of American Policy

Given his growing dependence on American military, political and economic support, Chiang could not afford to appear totally negative and disruptive. He must appear to offer a constructive alternative military strategy to that advocated by Stilwell. Adopting the old Chinese axiom of "playing the barbarians off against each other," the Generalissimo searched for a way to ingratiate himself with the President. He would do so by cooperating with those Americans who were jealous of or disagreed with Stilwell and who hoped to boost their own careers through working with the KMT. Chiang quickly discovered an antidote to Stilwell in the person of General Claire Chennault, former commander of the AVG and now leader of a small air task force in China.

Chennault deeply resented Stilwell's emphasis on a ground campaign, believing that air power held the key to victory in Asia. (It was his disciples who helped devise America's air strategy in Vietnam twenty years later.) Furthermore, the flier knew that only by winning more support for air warfare could he rise from his subordinate role in China. Chiang proved eager to accept Chennault's strategy because it served three basic needs at

once. If the very limited air freight capacity of the Hump transport route was filled with supplies (fuel, ammunition, spare
parts, etc.) for Chennault's air force, Stilwell would not be able
to accumulate stockpiles for his proposed Burma campaign.
Building up Chennault's power and prestige posed no threat to
Chiang since, unlike Stilwell, the flier virtually worshipped the
Generalissimo and Madame Chiang. Finally, permitting Chennault's warplanes to spearhead attacks against the Japanese in
China would cost Chiang no troops or resources but would still
create the popular illusion that China was the place where the
Japanese were really being fought. In return, the American peo-
ple would reward China with more aid.

Chennault lost no time in his effort to vault over Stilwell and
capture Roosevelt's attention. Distrustful of the War Department (where Chennault was considered a publicity hound), the
flier communicated directly with the President through a group
of carefully chosen intermediaries. Among the most important
was an aide to Chennault named Joseph Alsop, who happened
to be a distant cousin of the Roosevelts. Alsop and T. V. Soong
deluged the White House with advice on how to fight the war
in China. Calling Stilwell's policy a "national disgrace," they
claimed that if Chennault were given a handful of bombing
planes he could cripple Japanese forces in China and bring Japan to its knees. Never known for his modesty, Chennault asserted confidence that he could "not only bring about the downfall of Japan" but "make the Chinese lasting friends of the
United States." As icing on the cake, he promised to "create
such goodwill that China will be a great and friendly trade
market for generations." Who could ask for more?

Stilwell, naturally enough, despised both Chennault and his
ideas. Not only would they undercut his own army reform strategy, but they made no military sense. As soon as Chennault began his air attacks on Japanese forces and shipping, the Japanese
would attack his air bases. Since the Chinese army was a shambles, the bases could not possibly be defended. Unfortunately,
Stilwell's messages were not appreciated by the President. No
one in the White House wanted to hear caustic warnings about
the incompetence and weakness of America's ally. Chennault, on
the other hand, confided to Presidential aide Harry Hopkins and

others that if the administration supported an air war "there
was no doubt of success" in China. Chennault's supporters continually repeated the claim that an air strategy alone could win
the war and magically improve the political atmosphere in
Chungking.

All during 1942 and the first half of 1943 Stilwell labored in
vain to get Chiang and the reluctant British to begin a military
offensive in Burma. But without firm Presidential backing, there
was no way to compel the Chinese to do anything. In May 1943
the President sought to resolve this conflict of strategies by
having both Stilwell and Chennault present their cases directly
to him in Washington. The questions FDR asked the two competing generals were more concerned with politics than military
affairs. What did Stilwell think of Chiang? "He's a vacillating,
tricky, undependable old scoundrel who never keeps his word."
Chennault disagreed. "Sir, I think the Generalissimo is one of
the two or three greatest military and political leaders in the
world today."

The President had little interest in reading or analyzing the
detailed reports which Stilwell offered explaining the fallacies of
an air strategy. Chennault promised easy, cheap and quick success; Stilwell spoke of a protracted, difficult campaign which involved many military and political pitfalls. Not surprisingly,
Roosevelt resolved the dispute in favor of Chennault and decided to allocate the bulk of the precious supplies being flown
over the Hump to an air campaign. The President would even
have recalled Stilwell from China had not General Marshall and
Secretary of War Stimson continued to express their strong support for him.

The Rise and Fall of Air Warfare in China

The President's decision to indulge Chiang by shifting support
to Chennault reflected Roosevelt's belief that such actions were
a wise investment in future goodwill. Chiang should not be
forced to reform by threats, he told General Marshall in March
1943. It would be counterproductive to bully Chiang, a man
who had created in China "what it took us a couple of centuries

to attain." The Generalissimo was the "undisputed leader of 400,000,000 people" and could not be dictated to as Roosevelt might "the Sultan of Morocco."

By then Marshall understood why the President had been seduced by Chennault's absurd claims. It was not that anyone with a grain of military sense believed that air power alone could defeat Japan, but that Chiang wanted Chennault. As Marshall put it:

> Since the Chinese wanted what Chennault wanted, and Roosevelt wanted to give the Chinese what they wanted, all these things fit together very neatly and required no further presidential effort or analysis.

At a deeper level the President's actions in regard to China demonstrated how far American political leaders were divorced from the reality of the situation. In contrast to Roosevelt's sophisticated views of European rivalries and politics, he, and most of those around him, had only the dimmest comprehension of Chinese conditions. They failed to realize that Chiang's military policy overlay a deeper political crisis in China, that these problems could not be solved by indulging Chiang's whims. Furthermore, their unbounded (and unwarranted) faith that China's glorious future justified postponing the day of reckoning with Chiang insured that the KMT would undertake no reforms and thus hasten its own destruction.

Fully aware of how he had been cut adrift by Washington, a very bitter and disappointed Stilwell returned to China in the summer of 1943. His diary reflected overwhelming resentment felt toward Roosevelt, Chennault and Chiang. "Back again on the manure pile after that wonderful trip home. . . . Back to find Chiang the same as ever—a grasping, bigoted, ungrateful little rattlesnake."

For the next twelve months, until the spring of 1944, Stilwell bided his time, doing what little he could to reorganize his thirty Chinese divisions with the few resources that remained available. Chiang continued to interfere with all of Stilwell's training programs and came perilously close to beginning open warfare with the Chinese Communists. As much as possible, both Chiang and Stilwell labored to undercut each other's power base. The Generalissimo continued to complain to Washington about Stilwell, while Stilwell tried hard to channel American supplies to Chiang's many rivals within the KMT. He even dabbled in several plots to overthrow the KMT leader.

Meanwhile, Chennault gradually built up his forces until he was able to begin an air offensive late in 1943. The results proved devastating, but not exactly in the way Chennault had promised. As soon as the air attacks began to hurt the Japanese, they counterattacked and quickly overran Chennault's forward air bases. The Chinese armies supposedly protecting them dissolved into a rabble. The Japanese assault on previously unoccupied east China was so rapid that by the spring of 1944 it appeared that all China might be overrun. Thus, Stilwell had been proved correct in his predictions. The Japanese advance had finally exposed the military and political bankruptcy of the Chiang-Chennault strategy. In the process, however, it looked like all of China might fall.

The devastating military events sweeping over China in the spring and summer of 1944 had a great impact upon President Roosevelt. They not only confirmed Stilwell's predictions, but forced Roosevelt to question his own faith in Chiang Kai-shek. In fact, FDR had begun to reassess his policy the previous November when he met the Chinese leader face-to-face at the Cairo Conference. During several tense meetings, Chiang harangued FDR with demands for more economic aid—he wanted a billion dollars this time—and additional weapons. Incredibly, Chiang still refused to commit himself to a Burma campaign. The reluctance of both the British and Chinese to pursue the war in the Pacific with sufficient vigor (the British pushed a strategy designed to reconquer their own important colonies first) infuriated the President.

In marked contrast, when FDR went on to Teheran, Iran, in November 1943 to confer with the Soviet leader, Joseph Stalin, the Russians promised to enter the war against Japan after Hitler's defeat. The promise of Russian assistance, as well as mounting evidence that China would not offer any real help against Japan, caused Roosevelt to step back from his posture of offering Chiang all out support. At Cairo, FDR even quipped to Stilwell that if Chiang were deposed in a coup, the U.S. would support whoever was "next in line."

The President showed his rising ire by blocking new economic aid for China. Treasury Secretary Morgenthau had uncovered evidence of massive embezzlement by Chiang's family and insisted that before he would give China "another nickel" the crooks could "go jump in the Yangtze." The President and his advisors had begun to shed their illusions about Nationalist China. The process accelerated in April 1944 when Stilwell and a few of his new Chinese divisions which had been trained in India began fighting in Burma. Despite furious Japanese resistance, Chiang refused to permit the bulk of the new divisions in China to enter Burma. On April 10, FDR ordered that Chiang be threatened with a cutoff of aid unless he assisted Stilwell in Burma. Chiang quickly sent his troops into battle.

By May and June the Japanese were still on the offensive in China proper and the KMT armies were crumbling. Yet Chiang continued to hold large forces in reserve, claiming they must guard the Communists. Roosevelt used this excuse to initiate a new policy.

Roosevelt and Chiang: Ultimatum and Retreat

By June 1944 Roosevelt was convinced that unless Chiang were actively forced to enter the war against Japan, America's wartime and postwar strategies were doomed. Increasingly, it became clear that the only hope of unifying China was to revitalize the United Front, thus depriving Chiang of any excuse that he needed to guard the CCP and permitting America to tap the military strength of the Communist armies in north China. It was hoped that wartime unity might be carried past Japan's surrender and prevent the outbreak of civil war in China. With these concerns in mind, FDR sent Vice-President Henry Wallace to China in June 1944 with instructions to press Chiang to seek a negotiated settlement with the Communists. America, he implied, would help mediate the discussions.

Furthermore, Roosevelt insisted that an American observer

The Burma road into China. (National Archives)

mission be allowed passage to the Communist capital, Yenan. Among the President's motives, it seems, was a desire to put a little fear in Chiang's mind, to let him know that Washington realized there were alternative political leaders and groups in China. Also, if the U.S. could successfully mediate in China, Chiang could no longer use the excuse of a Communist threat to postpone fighting Japanese. Wallace's report to FDR testified to the administration's growing disillusionment with the KMT.

> Chiang, at best, is a short-term investment. It is not believed that he has the intelligence or political strength to run post-war China. The leaders of post-war China will be brought forward by evolution or revolution and it now seems more like the latter.

As the military situation in China continued to deteriorate, Stilwell seized the moment to suggest again that Chiang be ordered to give him full command powers. Stilwell wanted complete freedom to direct China's war effort and even to utilize Communist units. On July 4, 1944, the President approved a telegram to Chiang which warned that "the future of all Asia is at stake. . . ." Air power had failed and now Stilwell must be given "command of all Chinese and American forces . . . including the Communist forces."

As he had always done, Chiang struggled to survive by playing his rivals off against each other. Rather than refuse the President's orders—and risk the loss of American aid—he gave his conditional agreement. Stilwell would soon be given the power to command, but first the President should send a personal emissary to smooth relations between Chiang and Stilwell.

When General Marshall heard that FDR was prepared to accept Chiang's suggestion, he moved quickly. Marshall wanted to insure that the emissary would support Stilwell and not be a hatchet man like previous Roosevelt emissaries. Secretary of War Henry Stimson joined Marshall in proposing Patrick J. Hurley for the mission. Hurley, a Republican, former Secretary of War, oil company lawyer and Washington gadfly, had enjoyed good relations with Stilwell during an earlier meeting. Moreover, FDR was known to share confidence in him. At the time no one thought Hurley would have any important role to play.

After a brief stop in Moscow, Hurley arrived in Chungking on September 6, 1944. Roosevelt, apparently, had given Hurley verbal instructions to visit Moscow and secure a pledge from the Soviets not to aid the Chinese Communists. The President believed that if the Russians steered clear of China, the CCP would have no hope of outside support and a compromise between them and Chiang could more easily be arranged. Unless such a peaceful settlement were reached quickly, civil war was sure to break out which would devastate China and scuttle American designs for postwar Asia.

During the first week Hurley spent in China, the pace of events quickened. Believing he now enjoyed the President's full support, Stilwell began making arrangements to take over military command and "get arms to the Communists who will fight." After more prodding by Stilwell, FDR and General Marshall sent an ultimatum to Chiang which Stilwell personally delivered on September 19, 1944. The message declared that the time for stalling had passed and unless Stilwell were given complete power to command all Chinese troops, United States aid would be terminated. The end of U.S. support would almost certainly cause Chiang's regime to collapse.

Stilwell's glee in delivering the ultimatum to Chiang was voiced in his diary:

> Mark this day in red on the calendar of life. At long last, at very long last, F.D.R. has finally spoken plain words, and plenty of them, with a firecracker in every sentence. "Get busy or else." A hot firecracker. I handed this bundle of paprika to the Peanut and then sank back with a sigh. The harpoon hit the little bugger right in the solar plexus, and went right through him. It was a clean hit, but beyond turning green and losing the power of speech, he did not bat an eye. He just said to me, "I understand." And sat in silence jiggling one foot.

This victory proved very short lived, for as Stilwell prepared to lead Chinese forces, Hurley secretly took it upon himself to work with Chiang in getting rid of the tiresome American general. Hurley's behavior over the next year showed his complete belief in the need to sustain Chiang in power. He feared that if Chiang lost power, China would fall victim to the Chinese Communists or the Soviet Union. Thus, a man completely ignorant of actual conditions in China took it upon himself to insure that the United States would sustain Chiang against all challenges.

On September 24, 1944, Hurley joined Chiang and T. V. Soong in sending a message to FDR. All three agreed that the real problem in China was Stilwell. If only he were removed as a thorn in Chiang's side, the Kuomintang would be able to carry out everything Roosevelt desired of it.

When it seemed that FDR might be wavering in his decision, Hurley sent a pair of messages to the President on October 10, 1944. He argued that: "There is no other Chinese known to me who possesses as many of the elements of leadership as Chiang Kai-shek. Chiang Kai-shek and Stilwell are fundamentally incompatible." Later that day Hurley cabled Washington that Stilwell's only motive was vindictiveness.

> His one intention . . . to subjugate a man who has led a nation in revolution and who has led an ill-fed, poorly equipped, practically unorganized army against an overwhelming foe for seven years. My opinion is that if you sustain Stilwell in this controversy you will lose Chiang Kai-shek and possibly you will lose China with him. . . . America will have failed in China.

President Roosevelt was forced to choose between two extreme positions—that of sustaining Stilwell or firing him. Yet, Hurley's reports to the President seemed to offer an easy way out. This was important, for in just a few weeks the President faced election for a fourth term. He was running on his proven record as a war leader and planner for peace. To break with China or to be blamed for China's collapse on the eve of election was political dynamite. After all, it was Roosevelt who had done so much to convince Americans that Chiang was a hero. Furthermore, the President and those closest to him had no understanding of how desperately unstable China was. They still harbored a hope that with some additional American support Chiang might muddle through against the Japanese and be induced to accept a compromise with the Communists. Finally, Hurley made the decision simpler by telling the President repeatedly that Chiang would follow through on past promises only if Stilwell were removed. The choice, Hurley told him, was between a quarrelsome general and the "indispensable" leader of China.

Roosevelt made the expedient decision, issuing an order on October 18, 1944, that Stilwell be recalled. His successor was General Albert Wedemeyer, a man Stilwell despised as "the world's most pompous prick." In turn, Hurley was elevated to ambassador, replacing the career diplomat Clarence Gauss who had been critical of Chiang for years, to little avail. American aid would continue but the Chinese would not be required to appoint an American commander.

A final note of caution is worth mentioning in our discussion of General Stilwell. It is easy—too easy—to see him as a selfless hero and potential savior of China. When compared to Americans like Chennault and the U.S. naval officers who assisted the KMT secret police,* Stilwell seems almost saintly. His earthy, caustic diary makes wonderfully entertaining reading to a later generation. But there were grave problems in Stilwell's program, problems distinct from those caused by Chiang.

Beyond his idea of developing a strong efficient, American-oriented Chinese army, Stilwell had little to offer China. He knew the depth of China's poverty, understood the misery in which the average Chinese peasant lived and died. Yet, as a military officer, he had scarcely thought about how to help China in other than military ways. Even his army reforms focused on identifying and promoting efficient Chinese soldiers, soldiers who had a Kuomintang and class background like Chiang's. There is little reason to expect that the new Chinese army Stilwell planned to create would have any desire or ability to cope with China's profound social problems. In some ways, a "better" army might even have retarded the process of change since its officers could more successfully defend the selfish interest of the existing elite.

Twenty-five years later, in Vietnam, President Richard Nixon would announce a similar strategy. Now called "Vietnamization," it proposed to train a client army under close American supervision. The policy proved both a military and political disaster in Vietnam. There is no reason to suspect it would have worked any better in China. Neither Stilwell nor many of those around him understood that real change in China could not be brought about by foreign control, advice or reform. China was a volcano, about to explode in a revolution which would dwarf

---

* During the war a secret U.S. Navy group in China, not under Stilwell's control, worked with KMT Secret Police chief, Tai Li, to train anticommunist guerrillas. The naval officers bitterly opposed Stilwell and other Americans who sought to cooperate with anti-Chiang groups.

the violence of the Japanese invasion. The forces represented by the Kuomintang and Communists were far too large and complex for Americans to control. The Chinese had to find their own solutions. The United States either had to accept this or fight against China.

Selected Additional Readings

The frustrations experienced by the United States during its WWII alliance with the KMT are chronicled in both formal histories and revealing personal memoirs by leading participants. For the personal side see: Joseph W. Stilwell, *The Stilwell Papers*, New York: W. Sloane Assoc., 1948; Theodore White and Annalee Jacoby, *Thunder Out of China*, New York: W. Sloane Assoc., 1946; Graham Peck, *Two Kinds of Time*, Boston: Houghton Mifflin, 1967.

Among the historical studies of this period are: Barbara Tuchman, *Stilwell and the American Experience in China, 1911–1945*, New York: Macmillan, 1971; Michael Schaller, *The United States Crusade in China, 1938–1945*, New York: Columbia University Press, 1979; Herbert Feis, *The China Tangle*, Princeton, N.J.: Princeton University Press, 1953; Jonathan Spence, *To Change China: Western Advisors in China 1620–1960*, Boston: Little, Brown, 1969.

Two memoirs by Han Suyin provide a remarkable view of how the Chinese experienced the war years. See *Birdless Summer*, New York: Putnam, 1968, and *Destination Chungking*, Boston: Little, Brown, 1942.

5

The United States Confronts the Chinese Revolution, 1942-1949

The tumultuous, often bitter course of KMT-American relations during WWII formed only part of a larger Chinese drama. All along the ill-defined battle fronts of north, south and central China, the KMT and CCP continued their political and military struggle. The Communists, centered in their remote capital city of Yenan where they lived in caves dug out of the sandy hills, spent the war years struggling against Japan and unceasingly building a mass peasant army. In 1937 they could claim control of only a few thousand square miles, a million people, and an army of perhaps 80,000. Compared to the Nationalists their power was negligible. Eight years later, when Japan surrendered, the Communists commanded almost a million troops, occupied one-fourth of China, and governed 100 million people. In just another four years all China would be theirs.

How can we explain this dramatic reversal of fortunes? Many diverse factors, of course, led to the Nationalist debacle and the Communist victory. In a typically self-centered way, numerous Americans attributed this colossal event to the alleged "treason" of a handful of American diplomats. But the essential element behind the successful revolution was the opposite manner in which the KMT and CCP responded to the challenge of the Japanese invasion.

After the first year of the Sino-Japanese War (late 1938), Japanese troops occupied the parts of China most important to them, primarily the eastern one-third of the country on a line from Peking to Canton. Chiang withdrew his government and armies to the remote west, leaving the loyalty and fate of hundreds of millions of Chinese up for grabs. The Generalissimo's strategy seemed simple: he would "trade space for time" and wait for an American victory to rescue him. Meanwhile the Nationalists hoarded American money and weapons for eventual use against the Communists. But this strategy contained a fatal flaw. Communist organizers poured into the vacuum created by the Nationalists' retreat. They moved through the countryside, behind Japanese lines, and organized a peasant-guerrilla army which eventually swept on to victory over the KMT.

Chiang's flawed strategy was no simple oversight, but directly connected to the nature of the KMT regime. Successful guerrilla warfare required mobilizing and arming the rural masses. A guerrilla army would threaten not only the Japanese but the landlords and gentry, the social classes which comprised Chiang's staunchest supporters. Thus Chiang faced an insoluble dilemma: to win the peasants he must lose the landholders. By this refusal—or inability—to move against his traditional allies, Chiang became their hostage, doomed by the very people who had kept him in power!

Precisely those circumstances which paralyzed the KMT helped bring success to the Communists. At countless villages in occupied and unoccupied territory across the face of China, the Communists arrived to organize the peasants against the Japanese. They waved the banner of patriotism, throwing themselves enthusiastically into a campaign which the Nationalists had already largely deserted. A report by U.S. military intelligence summarized the process of what happened when Communist forces entered a village.

> . . . its retinue of propagandists, social and economic workers, school teachers . . . immediately started organizing and training the peasant masses for resistance through guerrilla warfare. Their central idea in all these efforts was that the social and economic level of the peasants had to be improved in order to maintain

morale and to instill among the people a will to resist Japan and
support their own armies.

At this stage the Communists avoided radical land reform and
class struggle, for they wanted to attract as broad a base of support as possible. They did, however, reduce rents and try to
redress the most serious peasant grievances against notorious
local landlords, usurers and bullies.

But the Communists did something more, something quite
revolutionary for China: they treated the peasants as valuable
human beings. Theodore White, who spent the war years in
China, believed that this was the secret of the Communists'
success.

> If you take a peasant who has been swindled, beaten and kicked
> about for all his walking days and whose father has transmitted to
> him an emotion of bitterness reaching back for generations—if you
> take such a peasant, treat him like a man, ask his opinion, let him
> vote for a local government, let him organize his own police . . .
> decide on his own taxes, and vote himself a reduction in rent and
> interest—if you do all that the peasant becomes a man who has
> something to fight for, and he will fight to preserve it against any
> enemy, Japanese or Chinese.

As White described it, once this process began it became a
sustained reaction. The Communists could offer to the peasant

> an army and a government that help him harvest, teach him to
> read and write and fight off the Japanese who raped his wife and
> tortured his mother. [He] develops a loyalty to the army and the
> government and to the party that controls them. He votes for that
> party, thinks the way that party wants him to think, and in many
> cases becomes an active participant.

Within countless Chinese villages the Communists gained
support by working with and for the poor peasants and small
landholders. Ignoring the rich and influential gentry, the CCP
sponsored local defense groups, agricultural cooperatives, educational programs and political discussions. The peasants became convinced of two things. Not only were the Communists
dedicated to the patriotic struggle against Japan, but the peasants themselves had a direct stake in the survival and victory of
the CCP. The party became their representative, the voice of

their demands for social and economic justice against the land-lord class. As a result, many joined the Red military forces as regular soldiers or part-time militia.

The Japanese responded to Communist guerrilla activities by visiting terrible retribution upon villages. The "Three-All Policy" of "Burn All, Kill All, Loot All" was applied to regions suspected of sympathizing with the Communists. But Japanese brutality, like that of the Nationalists who squeezed the last grain out of starving peasants in Honan, only won more converts for the Communist cause. Gradually, more and more areas had two governments: Japanese or KMT by day, Communist by night.

During the Second World War, the Communists began to win China and the Kuomintang to lose it. The Communist Party proclaimed that for China to be independent and great once again it must throw off the shackles of both foreign control and internal oppression. Revolution and nationalism would be har-nessed together as one force. Power, the Communists learned, would come from the hundreds of millions of poor peasants, not the favor of the wealthy elite or foreign patrons loaning money. By 1949, the Communists parlayed this new source of political power into control of all China.

Americans Meet the Chinese Communists, 1942–44

American leaders never fully understood or accepted the reality of the Chinese revolution. Washington's policy towards the Chi-nese Communists, with few exceptions, oscillated between indif-ference and profound hostility. The tendency either to disregard the importance of the CCP or see it as an agent of a "global" conspiracy had a dire impact on Sino-American relations.

When the United States joined the war against Japan in De-cember 1941, there had been little contact between American officials and the Chinese Communists. A handful of American journalists and adventurers such as Edgar Snow, T. A. Bisson, Agnes Smedley, Evans Carlson and Anna Louise Strong had journeyed to Communist territory and written favorable reports on what they saw. But such activities had little impact on mass opinion or government policy.

Official American views of the Chinese Communists before 1941 were a combination of uncertainty and hostility. Government "experts" on communism and China were baffled by the appeal of a Marxist-Leninist party to Asian peasants. While sometimes calling the CCP a party of "agrarian reformers," these same experts assumed that all communist movements were directly or indirectly controlled by the Soviet Union and were therefore puppets of Moscow. These rather harsh judgments eroded only gradually after 1941, as a group of extremely talented U.S. Foreign Service officers in the Chunking embassy reported extensively on Chinese communism, and as the CCP itself made friendly overtures to Americans.

Following Pearl Harbor many more Americans and much more military aid flowed into China. This presented new dangers and opportunities for the Communists. They hoped to prevent Chiang from using this aid against them and even thought it might be possible to win some for themselves. Fortunately for the Communists, one of their representatives in Chungking (permitted under the United Front agreement) was the urbane and talented Chou En-lai. Chou had a special affinity for Americans and charmed almost all those he met. He befriended and entertained foreign journalists, diplomats and soldiers, frequently asking them to his tiny apartment which was continually surrounded by KMT secret police. Many Americans came to look upon Chou and his staff as selfless heroes buried in the KMT lion's den.

Always a congenial host, Chou En-lai made a special point of inviting Americans to visit Yenan in either private or official capacities. Obviously, the Communists expected Americans to be pleased with what they found in Yenan—not a surprising assumption given the horrendous conditions in the Nationalist areas. The Communists had much to gain by improving their relationship with Washington. Not least of all, it would raise their image from that of regional rebels to an internationally recognized political movement which was part of the allied war effort.

During 1942 and 1943 some junior American diplomats in Chungking were enthusiastic about accepting Chou's offer to visit them. John S. Service (a member of the embassy staff and an advisor to Stilwell), for example, feared that both the Communists and Chinese "liberals" would come to hate the U.S. for its exclusive support of Chiang. In desperation or revenge, these groups might turn "toward friendship with Russia." Service and some of his colleagues argued the need to send Americans to Yenan to determine firsthand what these Chinese were really like.

> What is the form of their local government? How "Communistic" is it? Does it show any Democratic character or possibilities? Has it won the support of the people? How does it compare with the conditions . . . in Kuomintang China? . . . What is the military and economic strength of the Communists and what is their probable value to the Allied Cause?

Only an American observer team could discover answers to these vital questions, and without answers how could Washington possibly formulate an intelligent policy towards China?

During 1943 and 1944 Service and fellow diplomats John Davies and Raymond Ludden worried that America's alliance to Chiang was not only useless in the present war but might soon involve the U.S. in a conflict with the Chinese Communists. Moreover, American hostility or indifference would probably drive the Chinese Communists into a firm alliance with the Russians. These junior American officials, all of whom had a deep understanding of China, were convinced that nationalism would sweep over all of postwar Asia. Like Roosevelt, they hoped the United States could influence the direction of these movements. But to do so, Davies wrote, the United States must "move with the historical stream rather than fighting it."

These men believed the Communist variety of Chinese nationalism would eventually triumph in China, whether the U.S. liked it or not. It would be folly to support Chiang and oppose the Communists simply because of their revolutionary domestic policy. The U.S. could not prevent Chiang's defeat and would certainly embitter the Communists against America if it tried to do so. An alternative might be to step back from the Kuomintang and initiate political contacts with the Communists. Then, even if the Communists won the expected civil war, they might not bear resentment against America nor necessarily side with

the Soviet Union, America's potential rival for future influence
in Asia.

General Stilwell and members of the Office of Strategic Services (the OSS was the WWII predecessor of the CIA) had a
separate but parallel reason for interest in cooperation with the
Communists. After experiencing only frustration from the Nationalists, they were excited by the prospect of joining with the
dynamic Communist guerrilla forces in warfare against the
Japanese. Stilwell wrote that he had to judge the KMT and
CCP by what he saw: KMT "corruption, neglect, chaos . . .
trading with the enemy" and "a terrible waste of life, callous disregard for all the rights of men." "Communist program . . . reduce taxes, rents, interest. Practice what they preach." But not
until the summer of 1944 could anyone convince the President
to approve contacts with Yenan.

Just as the near defeat of China by Japan in 1938 first
prompted President Roosevelt to aid Chiang's regime, the renewed offensive of 1944 now pushed Roosevelt towards the
Communists. As the KMT armies in east China crumbled
(among other problems, Chiang cut off their supplies because
he questioned the loyalty of the commanders!), Roosevelt had
to wonder whether the Nationalists really could become a "Great
Power" in postwar Asia. Prudently, FDR considered alternative
ways to preserve a vestige of stability. One idea was to bring the
Communists into the regime as a "junior partner" while limiting
Russian involvement in China. Moscow, FDR believed, could
be brought along by granting the Soviets special privileges in
Manchuria. Though imposing these policies contradicted his
public rhetoric about treating China as a "Great Power," they
promised to preserve at least a modicum of noncommunist
power in China. As early as the Teheran Conference of November 1943, Stalin and Roosevelt discussed exchanging railroad
and port privileges in Manchuria for Soviet support of Chiang.
The Yalta agreements of February 1945 eventually confirmed
the deal.

In pursuit of better relations with the Chinese Communists,
two groups of Americans breached the KMT blockade of Yenan
during the summer of 1944. A group of journalists arrived first.
After three years of witnessing the squalid conditions of "free"

China, these Americans found Yenan a remarkable improvement over Chungking. Their articles reflected strong approval of what they saw. Virtually all felt the people were "better fed, huskier and more energetic than in other parts of China." The local government actually helped the peasants, it did not simply tax them. Brooks Atkinson, the *New York Times* correspondent, believed the soldiers of the Communists' 8th Route Army were "among the best-clothed and best fed this writer has seen anywhere in China." Another reporter commented that an Allied Commander "would be proud to command these tough, well-fed, hardened troops." In the words of one journalist, Yenan was a "Wonderland City." When we remember that the Communists accomplished this with no foreign aid and in one of the poorest parts of China, the achievement is all the more remarkable. Unfortunately, KMT press censors were so frightened by these reports that they rewrote the copy before it reached the United States. Having learned a lesson, the Nationalists refused to allow any more reporters through the blockade.

The first *official* American observers entered Communist territory late in July 1944 following Roosevelt's unsuccessful attempt to pressure Chiang to reform. Calling themselves the "Dixie Mission" because they were in "rebel territory," this group included about two dozen technical personnel, political analysts and guerrilla warfare experts. Their presence enabled American officials to obtain first-hand knowledge about the Communists and permitted the Communists a chance to question and influence the Americans.

The Dixie Mission quickly took on a life of its own. Foreign Service officer John Service's first dispatch said it all. "We have come into a different country and are meeting a different people." The Communists were similarly excited by the mission. They obviously hoped it would allow them to leap over Chiang's military blockade and secure some form of U.S. political recognition and military aid.

Between July and November, 1944, the Communists treated the Americans in Yenan as valued friends. The top CCP leaders hobnobbed with junior American diplomats and soldiers. Mao Tse-tung, in particular, questioned Service about American policy and attitudes. According to Mao, the U.S. had nothing to

fear from the Communists. "Even the most conservative American businessman can find nothing in our program" to object to,
he claimed. During detailed conversations, Mao admitted how
vulnerable the Communists were to American policy:

> America does not need to fear we will not cooperate. We must
> cooperate and we must have American help. This is why it is
> important to us Communists to know what you Americans are
> thinking and planning. We cannot risk crossing you—cannot risk
> conflict with you.

In many conversations during the last few months of 1944 the
Communist leaders referred to their own tenuous position vis à
vis the KMT, the United States and the Soviet Union. While
fighting both Japan and the Nationalists, the Communists were
also absorbed in developing their strategy for agrarian revolution. Mao's ongoing purge of CCP members with a background
of Soviet training confirmed the uneasy relationship between
Moscow and Yenan. For the short term, at least, improved relations with the United States seemed vital if the Communists
were to face a civil war with no promise of Russian assistance.
No one who met Mao could doubt the sincerity of his nationalism nor his determination to make China a "great power." Yet
this new China could still be a stable nation, a major trading
partner and an important counterweight to possible Soviet expansion in Asia. The Communists did not deny their commitment to a Chinese revolution. But they did constantly assert the
belief that a communist China need not threaten American
interests.

With their belief that Yenan and Washington had certain
parallel interests in China, the Communists steadfastly pursued
American favor from the autumn of 1944 through the following
summer. Determined to resist both the Japanese and Kuomintang, they maintained hope of receiving military and political
assistance from the United States. Under the right circumstances, they declared, they would even be willing to form a
temporary coalition with the Nationalists. In the long run,
neither the Communists nor the Americans could guess how
cooperation might affect their two countries. But in late 1944

it certainly seemed that a radical change from the hostility and indifference of the past could not make matters worse.

As these political discussions took place, several OSS officers in Yenan began to offer the Communists basic instruction in the use of some donated American weapons. These individual acts convinced the Communists that U.S. policy was really beginning to turn around, about to rid itself of dependence on Chiang and consider cooperation with Yenan. By September 1944, reports of General Stilwell's plans to send military aid to the Communists further bolstered this belief.

This cooperation never came to pass. At that very moment Chiang Kai-shek and Patrick J. Hurley, Roosevelt's special emissary to China, were conspiring to convince FDR to fire Stilwell and maintain a policy of aid to the Kuomintang exclusively. Henceforth, both Hurley and the President sought to contain the crisis in China by pressuring the Communists into accepting a minor role in a KMT-dominated government. Simultaneously they cut Yenan off from any support from either sympathetic Americans or the Soviet Union.

This drama was first played out by Hurley soon after Stilwell's recall in October 1944. On November 7, 1944, without any prior announcement, Hurley flew to Yenan. As he stepped off the American plane to be met by the American commander of the Dixie Mission and Chou En-lai, the CCP leader was shocked to learn that this unexpected visitor was Roosevelt's emissary. "Keep him here until I can find Chairman Mao," Chou said, and he dashed off to town.

Hurley (who privately referred to CCP leaders Mao Tse-tung and Chou En-lai as "Moose Dung and Joe N. Lie") shocked everyone by uttering a bloodcurdling Choctaw Indian war cry as he deplaned. It proved only the first of many bizarre outbursts. Not surprisingly, the Communists soon referred to Hurley as "the Clown." At first the Communists and Hurley got on unexpectedly well. He pleased Mao by promising that if the CCP leader went to Chungking for peace talks, the U.S. would guarantee a generous compromise settlement with the KMT. Political power and U.S. aid would be shared. The Communists would be recognized as a part of a new coalition government. After

Mao and Hurley signed a "Five Point" draft agreement to this effect, Chou En-lai accompanied Hurley back to Chungking in mid-November.

What happened next proved a rude awakening for the Communists. At first it seemed that Hurley might fulfill the hopes raised in Yenan by the presence of the Dixie Mission. Instead, when Chou met with Chiang Kai-shek he was handed a note demanding that the Communists dissolve their independent armies and accept some token political appointments to the KMT government. No one familiar with the previous twenty years could doubt that surrender of their troops would mean mass suicide for the Communists. Negotiations ended abruptly on November 21, 1944, and shortly thereafter an embittered Chou En-lai returned to Yenan. The Communists realized that Hurley had lied to them, for now he too demanded that the Communists forget the earlier compromise draft agreement and accept Chiang's suicide proposal.

Hurley responded to this breakdown of negotiations by attacking those Americans who had been sympathetic to Yenan. If the Communists' American friends were forced out of China, he reasoned, the CCP would have no hope of relying on foreign support. They would be forced to accept Chiang's—and Hurley's—terms. Realizing what Hurley intended, and hopeful that the President might countermand his actions, Mao and Chou undertook a daring maneuver: a secret approach to FDR which would circumvent Hurley's influence.

On January 9, 1945, the Communists asked that members of the Dixie Mission forward a secret cable to Roosevelt. Mao and Chou offered to travel to Washington to meet the President and make a personal appeal for American support. Clearly, the Communists still believed that at the highest levels American policy remained flexible, that they could still cooperate with the United States, both against Japan and in the search for a political compromise.

Nothing worked the way Mao and Chou hoped. Hurley quickly learned of the "secret" message and warned FDR against dealing with the CCP. The Communists, he declared, were responsible for all China's problems and were refusing to reach a fair settlement with the KMT because disloyal Americans had joined them in a "conspiracy" against Chiang and Roosevelt. Hurley's message to FDR gave birth to the charge that American "spies" or "traitors" were somehow in league with the Chinese Communists working to oppose U.S. interests.

Roosevelt, who was already preoccupied with political and military problems surrounding the imminent end of the war in Europe, declined to reevaluate his own or Hurley's actions. Instead, FDR backed Hurley and authorized the removal from China of any American whom the egotistical ambassador considered "disloyal." Hurley defined disloyalty as any questioning of Chiang's wisdom or virtue, or any willingness to support Yenan. Over the next several months Hurley made members of his staff swear their loyalty to his own policy and even threatened to shoot one junior diplomat who had the courage to criticize Chiang. Those who did not toe the ambassador's line were sent home or as some put it, "Hurleyed out of China."

The President's New Policy: Yalta

By February 1945 Roosevelt must have begun to realize that his dream of fathering a "powerful, united and pro-American China" was fast becoming a nightmare. At best, China might be held together in a tenuous KMT-CCP alliance. But civil war appeared likely and this raised the prospect of prolonged instability in the Far East, creating a vacuum which might entice Soviet penetration. To increase the chance of maintaining a Kuomintang-dominated China, Roosevelt finally sought the active cooperation of the Soviet dictator, Joseph Stalin. (By then Stalin, too, had added "Generalissimo" to his impressive string of titles.)

Ever since he emerged as the ruler of the Soviet Union in the late 1920s, Stalin had revealed a curious attitude towards foreign, and especially Chinese, communists. Beneath the public facade of Russian support for all revolutionary movements was the reality of Stalin's cautious attitude in foreign affairs. The Russian leader assisted communist movements when they were under his personal control or served what he believed were the best interests of the Soviet Union (for Stalin these were often the same). Stalin followed a very ambivalent policy towards Chinese communism. He realized that although Mao and his followers had built a popular, strongly nationalistic revolutionary movement, they did not accept the Soviet Union as their master or model. The prospect of a powerful, independent Communist China bordering Russia was not necessarily a pleasant vision for the security-conscious Soviet leader. In fact, during the late 1930s, as in the 1920s, Stalin had given substantial military aid to the KMT as the Chinese group best able to resist Japanese expansion. In many ways, the maintenance of a KMT regime with loose or partial control over China would pose less of a potential challenge to the Soviet Union than would a powerful communist neighbor. American observers in Yenan in 1944–45 carefully noted that only a handful of Russians resided in the Communist capital and they were not on close terms with the CCP leaders.

In February 1945 the leaders of Great Britain, the United States and the Soviet Union conferred at Yalta, in the Soviet Crimea, to arrange the future of liberated Europe. Complicated discussions concerning what type of political order should be established in Eastern Europe and Germany frustrated Roosevelt, Stalin and Churchill. FDR saw little alternative to conceding control of Eastern Europe to the Soviets. But, the President seemed to believe, he could trade this concession for Stalin's commitment to a stable world order.

In their discussion of the Far East and Russian entry into the war against Japan (something very much desired by the Americans) Stalin told Roosevelt he would support Chiang's regime and ignore the Chinese Communists. He did, however, insist that the Soviet Union acquire special rights to share control of the major railroads and ports of Manchuria. Believing this was a relatively small price to pay to keep the Soviets out of China, Roosevelt agreed to press Chiang to concede what Stalin demanded in Manchuria. Although many later observers bitterly criticized the President for the Yalta agreements, FDR gave up virtually nothing that the Russians would not have acquired anyway. Russian troops would certainly enter Manchuria after Germany's defeat and it seemed prudent to set limits on the scope of Soviet expansion. Moreover, a Nationalist China minus parts of Manchuria seemed a far better deal than conceding nothing and risking Soviet intervention on behalf of the CCP.

Roosevelt's revised policy of supporting Chiang and securing a Soviet promise to do the same might have succeeded if the Chinese Communists had not been the independent group they claimed to be. Mao and his followers would not give up their struggle simply because they had been denied American and Soviet support. They might still be willing to share power with Chiang, but they would certainly not surrender their own armies and enter a coalition as a powerless member as Roosevelt and Stalin suggested. Also, the American failure to restrain the KMT convinced Chiang he could be more recalcitrant and uncompromising than ever. After all, he now appeared to enjoy *both* American and Soviet backing! Although Roosevelt still spoke in favor of a compromise in China, so long as U.S. aid flowed only to the KMT, and Ambassador Hurley and General Wedemeyer openly supported Chiang, no *real* compromise was possible.

By the spring of 1945 the Communists had lost almost all hope of influencing American policy. In March John Service rejoined the Dixie Mission's fast diminishing ranks and heard Mao plead for a reversal of Washington's course. The Communist leader lamented that ever since December 1944 American policy had veered away from compromise. Hurley's hostile actions would ensure that "all that America has been working for will be lost." Mao emphasized the great significance of American aid and pointedly declared that: "There is no such thing as America not intervening in China! You are here as China's greatest ally. The fact of your presence is tremendous."

Service and most other Americans in China pleaded with their superiors to reconsider their course and rebuke Hurley. On February 28 (while the unpopular ambassador was en route to Washington) they sent a joint telegram to the State Department warning that current policy would encourage civil war and drag the U.S. in as a KMT ally. The embassy staff hoped to "point out the advantage of having the Communists helped by the United States rather than seeking Russian aid or intervention, direct or indirect." Solomon Adler, a Treasury Department official serving in China spoke even more directly. America's future in China, he wrote, "should not be left in the hands of a bungler like Hurley."

These warnings, however graphic, were outweighed by the arguments presented by Hurley and Wedemeyer during their visit to Washington in March 1945. The two senior American officials in China denied every criticism of their support for Chiang. They described the Communists as a weak, unpopular and hostile group responsible for China's turmoil. Chiang, they claimed, could easily "put down the communist rebellion" and control all China if only the U.S. would give him more support. Weary and only a few weeks away from his death, President Roosevelt declined to rebuke Hurley and actually effusively praised his behavior of the past few months. The formal confirmation of the anticommunist policy came on April 2, 1945, when Hurley emerged from a meeting with the President in Washington and in a public news conference denounced the CCP as largely responsible for blocking peace in China. By implication, even Roosevelt had now abandoned an evenhanded policy.

American-Communist Hostility:
June to August, 1945

The Chinese Communists reacted to these events by lambasting Hurley and other anonymous American "reactionaries" who, they said, plotted civil war in China. When Mao addressed the CCP Congress in Yenan in April 1945 he warned that the Americans and the KMT were jointly planning to attack the Communists in the wake of Japan's defeat. Communist fear accelerated in June when word came from Washington that John Service, the Foreign Service officer, had been arrested on espionage charges for passing classified documents to *Amerasia* magazine. The arrest of the American most trusted by the CCP was interpreted as proof of a growing anticommunist plot in Washington. (Although Service was eventually acquitted of all charges, the complex case left a stain on his reputation and eventually was used by pro-KMT forces in Congress to hound him out of the

State Department.) Yenan's reaction to the incident appeared in radio and press messages beamed to America: If the American imperialists did not "withdraw their hands . . . then the Chinese people will teach them a lesson they deserve." These denunciations of American policy grew in intensity as the war in the Pacific drew to a close.

Hurley's actions in China and the growing anticommunist attitude in Washington were part of a general trend in American policy during the late spring of 1945. Roosevelt's death in mid-April accelerated the deterioration of the Grand Alliance. While the U.S. and Soviet Union would certainly have experienced major tensions and disagreements even had FDR lived, his passing removed one of the few American leaders determined to try to get along with the Soviets.

Harry S. Truman assumed the presidency with remarkably little preparation and virtually no understanding of international relations. He knew nothing about the development of the atomic bomb nor did he know very much about the complicated diplomatic arrangements worked out between FDR and Stalin. Understandably, this insecure and inexperienced leader relied upon people he presumed to be the experts. Roosevelt's leading advisors on foreign policy were generally far more hostile to the Soviet Union than the President himself had been. They interpreted Russian demands for security and retribution against Germany, as well as Stalin's insistence on the creation of pro-soviet regimes in Eastern Europe, as preludes to global communist expansion. Only a tough, assertive policy, they argued, could limit Stalin's grasp.

Turning their gaze towards Asia, they saw Soviet interest in Manchuria and the rise of Chinese Communist power as a copy of the situation in Europe. Most American officials neither understood nor believed that Communist strength in China was the product of local conditions. Influential spokesmen on foreign affairs, such as the future Secretary of State John Foster Dulles, argued vehemently in favor of sustaining the Nationalists. The essence of U.S. policy, he told an audience in early 1945, was a "determination that the 400,000,000 of China shall not become harnessed to the predatory design of an alien power." Chiang had chosen to "rely on the ultimate support of the Christian democracies, notably the United States." To desert him would be akin to sin.

One of the most articulate and influential of the circle of advisors around the new President was Averell Harriman, then ambassador to the Soviet Union. In discussions with the conservative Secretary of the Navy James Forrestal, Harriman identified China as one of several flash points where international communism had resolved to challenge the United States. If the United States wavered in its duty to support Chiang, he warned, "we should have to face ultimately the fact that two or three hundred millions of people would march when the Kremlin ordered." Harriman's vivid imagery confirmed that the highest circle of American leaders had come to view the Chinese Communists as Russian agents totally hostile to the United States. It was not hard to convert this illusion into a self-fulfilling prophecy.

By July 1945 the entire orientation of U.S. foreign policy had taken on an anti-Soviet and antirevolutionary posture. American leaders no longer saw the Soviet Union as a loyal ally against Germany and a future ally against Japan. Instead, the Russians had become the new threat to world peace, a totalitarian and fanatical nation plotting the conquest of Western Europe and Asia.

The Potsdam Conference, held in conquered Berlin late in July 1945, revealed how far apart the Russians and Americans had grown. Each side accused the other of breaking wartime promises on the division of Germany, the payment of reparations and the political future of Eastern Europe. However, since Russian military help against Japan still seemed necessary, Truman's advisors counselled the President against a total break with Stalin.

Then, in the midst of the Potsdam meeting, American scientists successfully detonated the atomic bomb in New Mexico. This new weapon yielded immediate military and political results. Japan might now be defeated quickly, without Russian assistance. Furthermore, if Russia were kept out of the war, it would probably limit Soviet penetration of Manchuria, where millions of Japanese troops remained. As Truman's new Secretary of State, James F. Byrnes put it, the atomic bomb might get Japan to "surrender before Russia goes into the war and this will save China. If Russia goes into the war . . . Stalin will take over and China will suffer." Thus, by the end of July 1945, American leaders hoped to end the Pacific war quickly, perhaps even before the Russians could enter China and assist the Chinese Communists. As Truman told a group of naval officers in July, with the atomic bomb "we did not need the Russians or any other nation."

Despite these overwhelming American fears, Stalin appeared to have no grandiose scheme in China. While the Russians hoped to dominate parts of Manchuria and seize Japanese-built industry there, they seemed unprepared to assist the rise of the Chinese Communists. Stalin pushed for concessions from Chiang which would have benefited Russia more than FDR had hoped. But these benefits would not help the CCP. On August 14, hours before Japan's surrender, Stalin and T. V. Soong reached an agreement on a Sino-Soviet treaty to implement the Yalta accords. In exchange for receiving special railroad and port privileges in Manchuria, the Soviets pledged their "moral, material, and military support to China and solely to the Chinese National Government" led by Chiang. When word of this treaty reached Yenan, the Communists seemed stunned and despondent, American observers noted. Stalin, like the American leaders, appeared to favor a weak KMT regime to the uncertainties of a Communist China or one wracked by civil war.

The Japanese Surrender and American Intervention: August to November, 1945

The Japanese surrender of August 14, 1945, following the use of two atomic bombs and a Soviet assault on Manchuria, brought peace to America and a bloody four-year civil war to China. The smoldering hostility, only partially restrained by the United Front since 1937, burst again into flames. A crucial element of both Communist and Nationalist strategy was to seize quickly the huge amount of territory and weapons held by the more

than three million Japanese and puppet troops in China. Which-
ever side acquired these resources would have a major military
advantage, a fact which Washington thoroughly understood.

Immediately upon Japan's surrender, President Truman issued "General Order #1," a command that all Japanese and
puppet forces in China surrender their positions and arms only
to Chiang Kai-shek or his representatives. Truman, by this decision, put American support even more directly behind the KMT.
Though the Communist leaders denounced this as a betrayal of
their wartime role against Japan and declared their intention of
ignoring General Order #1, Washington brushed aside all pro-
tests.

To assist unreliable or scarce KMT troops, almost 60,000
American Marines were rushed from the Pacific to be rede-
ployed along vital rail lines, ports and airfields in north China.
In addition, the American navy and air forces ferried hundreds
of thousands of KMT soldiers from south to north China. All of
this intervention was justified by the claim that American forces
were helping to disarm and repatriate the surrendered Japanese.
In fact, both American and KMT forces cooperated with the
"surrendered" Japanese in resisting Communist efforts to seize
cities and lines of communication. The enemy army of only
weeks before was now a valued ally! One disgruntled Marine
complained of this in a letter to a Senator:

> We were told when en route to [north China] that we were to
> assist in the disarming of Japanese troops in this area. Before we
> arrived, the Chinese had the situation well in hand, and have since
> gone so far as to re-arm some Japanese units for added protection
> against Chinese Communist forces. Recently we have been told
> that the reason for our prolonged visit is to hold the area in lieu
> of the arrival of General Chiang Kai-shek's Nationalist forces. In
> other words we are here to protect General Chiang's interests
> against possible Communist uprisings. Everything we do here
> points directly or indirectly toward keeping the Chinese Com-
> munists subdued.

In addition to the Marines and transportation provided to the
KMT armies, the level of United States military Lend-Lease to
the Nationalist regime actually increased in the six months

following Japan's surrender. More aid arrived after the war was over—several billion dollars' worth—than had been given to Chiang for use against Japan.*

In light of this massive American aid to Chiang and the Soviet Union's general indifference, Yenan faced a difficult choice. An immediate civil war favored the KMT. It seemed advantageous to postpone battle until the Communists could mobilize and expand their forces. Since the Americans still argued that the Communists should join the KMT in a coalition, in late August Mao agreed to explore again the possibility of a compromise. Whatever his misgivings about the American-KMT alliance, Mao felt that it was crucial to delay full-scale fighting.

The new peace talks in Chungking broke down almost as soon as they began. Chiang, with Hurley's approval, repeated his position that coalition required a virtual Communist surrender—no sharing of power or territorial partition. This "hard line" appealed to Chiang, Hurley and Truman's advisors because the initial developments following Japan's surrender seemed to favor the KMT's military position heavily.

But as fighting spread through north China during the autumn months this optimism began to fade. While KMT forces seized urban centers, Communist guerrilla forces controlled the countryside and began to isolate the Nationalist positions. If America was to help Chiang, it would have to do far more on his behalf than had been anticipated. Washington faced the dilemma of whether to expand the American military effort in China or leave Chiang to his own fate.

While Ambassador Hurley demanded a wider involvement, other American policymakers voiced renewed doubts about his advice and Chiang's competence. From China General Wedemeyer wrote that Chiang had little hope of unifying China without direct American intervention. Truman and his advisors had no sudden fondness for the Chinese Communists. But they were forced to admit that the CCP seemed able to hold its own against all of Chiang's military efforts. The only way they might be defeated was to dispatch a huge American combat force to

---

* Soviet forces in Manchuria turned over stockpiles of captured Japanese weapons to Communist troops, though the policy varied and the scope of aid was much smaller than U.S. assistance to the KMT.

China, something which the KMT hoped for and almost everyone in Washington opposed as reckless. The President, like his foreign policy experts, believed the main problem facing the U.S. was the threat they perceived coming from the Soviet Union in Eastern Europe. This sense sharply affected—as it would through the ensuing decade—American policies and capabilities in China. Reluctantly, by November 1945, the Truman Administration concluded that the deteriorating military situation in China could only be reversed if the United States again sought to mediate a coalition settlement.

The Administration's plans were jolted on November 27 when Ambassador Hurley (then in Washington) called a public news conference to announce his resignation. Obviously fearful his own policy would be labeled a failure, Hurley, with his accustomed flamboyance, blamed all China's troubles on the actions of "spies" and "traitors" in the State Department who were linked to the Communists. Although false, these charges eventually took on a life of their own. After 1949, when a scapegoat had to be found to explain the Communist victory in China, the charges of treason were revived against those farsighted diplomats who had warned against supporting Chiang.

The Marshall Mission and the Failure of Mediation

Hoping both to defuse Hurley's slanderous charges and perhaps salvage some American influence in China, President Truman appointed General George C. Marshall to lead a new peace effort. Marshall's Mission (December 1945–January 1947) strove to get the KMT and CCP to agree to a cease-fire to be followed by the creation of a coalition government. This basically followed the pattern which Roosevelt had pursued during the war. However, according to the orders sent by the Secretaries of State, War, and Navy to General Wedemeyer one day after Hurley's resignation, America would continue to provide "at least indirect support of Chiang Kai-shek's activities against dissident forces in China." Truman and Marshall agreed that if the Communists refused to make "reasonable concessions," the Americans would openly assist Chiang's armies in their movement to the disputed parts of China. The United States could not tolerate "a divided China" or the "resumption of Russian power in Manchuria." To prevent this, Washington "would have to swallow its pride and much of its policy" and continue to assist the KMT, lamented Marshall.

Thus, even in their desire to forestall civil war, American leaders were still reluctant to admit the deeper sources of the Chinese revolution. They had the greatest difficulty in distinguishing social revolution and radical nationalism from Soviet expansion. Truman and Marshall believed that it was necessary to preserve "order" and "stability" in China as a way to block Moscow. They tended to interpret the contending forces as proxies connected to the rivalry between Moscow and Washington. The American goal in China after 1945 became the prevention of revolutionary change linked to global Soviet expansion.

Though they must have been quite wary of its sincerity, the Communists hailed the Marshall Mission as an important "change in American policy." From the Communists' perspective, postponing civil war was clearly preferable to an immediate showdown with the better equipped and larger KMT armies. In December 1945, Chou En-lai and a Communist delegation returned to Chungking and prepared to begin negotiations with Chiang and Marshall. The tone of the talks, however, was set by what occurred on the airfield as Marshall's plane was about to touch down. KMT police "started to chase the Communist representatives off the field" and the delegates were only rescued by the intervention of American diplomats.

Marshall's initial discussions with the two warring groups disclosed very little room for compromise. The Communists insisted that in any coalition they share real power and maintain their separate army; Chiang declared that the Communists must be disarmed and accept whatever political crumbs he might offer. For his part, within his self-imposed limitations, Marshall strove to be evenhanded. Without promising either side anything, the American mediator arranged for a cease-fire in contested parts of north China and Manchuria. Three-party truce teams were established to enforce the peace. On July 29, 1946, Marshall placed an embargo on arms shipments to China and hastened the removal of American Marines. Yet, these restraints on the KMT were undercut by the extension of additional aid to Chiang. For example, a special surplus property agreement transferred huge stocks of American military equipment already in China to the Nationalists.

During the latter half of 1946 the cease-fire came apart as both sides took advantage of the other's weaknesses. Chiang, especially, remained convinced that in any showdown Washington would stand by his government. The Communists, who viewed with growing alarm the American hostility towards both the Soviet Union and virtually all revolutionary movements in Asia and Europe, lost faith in Marshall's impartiality. In January 1947, as civil war flared across China, Truman called his unsuccessful mediator home to assume the post of Secretary of State. Marshall departed with a verbal blast at both the KMT and CCP. The end of the mission seemed to be Washington's acknowledgement that there was no American solution for China. That nation would have to find its own path through civil war to peace.

Civil War to Liberation

Almost three years passed between Marshall's departure and the creation of the Communist People's Republic of China. Initially Chiang's American-equipped armies seemed far superior to the guerrillas and peasant militia which the Communists had organized during the War of Resistance. But in truth, as one American general put it, the KMT troops suffered from "the world's worst leadership." They were routed from positions which they might have "defended with broomsticks" if they had the will. Not just military tactics but morale and politics dictated the outcome of the civil war. A French military expert concluded that, as much as anything else, the maladministration and corruption of the KMT civil administration destroyed civilian morale which directly affected the quality of the Nationalist armies.

> . . . the Nationalist soldier . . . was generally considered to be the scum of humanity. Except in several elite divisions, such a conception could not be changed and morale remained low despite

promised reforms. . . . the soldier of Chiang Kai-shek knew not why he fought. Against the Japanese he could fight for his country and his people; but in this civil war a peasant soldier from Kwangtung had no idea why he should be fighting in Shansi and Manchuria. Poorly fed, poorly paid, poorly clothed, poorly cared for, poorly armed, often short of ammunition—even at decisive moments—unsustained by any faith in a cause, the Nationalist soldier was easy prey for the clever and impassioned propaganda of the Communists.

The Kuomintang not only squandered its military advantage but managed to alienate almost all segments of Chinese society in the years 1945–49. During the reoccupation of China from the Japanese, KMT civil and military officers indulged themselves in an orgy of personal aggrandizement. They seized for personal use public property and land, connived with collaborators, ignored the most fundamental economic problems and disregarded public sentiment calling for a compromise with the CCP which would stop the bloodshed of the civil war. In the countryside the KMT again relied on the landlord class as its agents, further alienating the peasants.

The more selfish and blundering the KMT became, the more flexible and popular the Communist program seemed to become. During the civil war the CCP continued to press two great battles at once: the first against the KMT, the second against the social structure of the Chinese village. As they had begun to do behind Japanese lines, Communist organizers infiltrated villages and aroused the fury of the poor peasant against the rich, the debtor against the usurer, the exploited against the exploiter. This campaign of land and social reform not only created a mass base of rural support for the Communists but served as their recruiting headquarters for new troops. By 1948, in Manchuria and on the north China plain, the military initiative passed to the revolutionary armies. Nationalist garrisons, deserted and isolated, began to fade away and surrender.

As the civil war dragged on, China became an increasingly partisan topic in American politics. In 1947 the Truman Administration came under attack for its supposed "softness" on communism. A group of Republican Senators and Congressmen criticized Truman for having first sponsored the idea of including the Communists in a coalition government and then, after Marshall's departure, for not doing enough to help Chiang defeat the Communists. At the same time many of the most qualified China specialists in the State Department were accused of disloyalty. The same men who had correctly warned of Chiang's weakness and the Communists' strength were now blamed for causing the disaster overtaking the KMT. Here was another example of punishing the messenger who brought the bad news. The charges of disloyalty and subversion, initiated by Ambassador Hurley upon his resignation, were perpetuated by the "China Lobby," an assortment of individuals and groups rumored to be financed by the KMT.

The Truman Administration was forced on the defensive over China partly because it had succeeded so well in selling the doctrine of "containment" to the public. Between 1947 and 1949 Truman sponsored the Truman Doctrine, the Marshall Plan and the NATO military alliance, all designed to shore up Europe against Communist encroachment by extending military and economic assistance. Chiang's supporters in both parties and among the public wondered why the possible triumph of Chinese communism was not resisted as vociferously as the "threat" in Europe. The Truman Administration never directly answered this question, leaving its critics free to snipe and ridicule with impunity.

The make-believe world in which Chiang's American allies resided was demonstrated by their complete misunderstanding of Chinese politics. In May 1947, *Time* ran a cover story featuring Ch'en Li-fu, one of Chiang's most notoriously reactionary aides. According to *Time* Ch'en was a virtual reincarnation of the sage Confucius, struggling to build a new China within the Confucianist framework. Ambitious Congressmen, Senators and journalists discovered that "China" was a hot political issue. Since few people knew much about the real conditions there, almost anyone could claim to be a "China-expert." The Republican Party, longing for an issue on which to attack the Democrats who had been in power since 1933, perfected the art of baiting the Administration on China.

Many of the most ardent defenders of Chiang in Congress were demagogues who simply exploited the issue. Senators William F. Knowland, Styles Bridges, Owen Brewster, Pat McCarran (a Democrat) and Kenneth Wherry eventually came to be known as "the Senators from Formosa." In the House, Congressmen Richard Nixon and George Dondero beat the drum for Chiang ceaselessly. Truman's most vociferous critic in Congress was a representative from Minnesota, Walter Judd, who had once been a medical missionary in China. Senator Kenneth Wherry, one of Chiang's more hysterical boosters, revealed his own arrogance and ignorance by explaining America's duty towards China: "With God's help," he declared, the United States could "lift Shanghai up and up, ever up, until it is just like Kansas City."

Even better educated and more talented members of Congress saw advantage in red-baiting the Administration over China. In 1949 Congressman John F. Kennedy delivered a blistering attack against leaders who had sacrificed China and Chiang to communism. The Administration had deserted China, he claimed, "whose freedom we once fought to preserve. What our young men had saved, our diplomats and President have frittered away." Kennedy, too, suggested that a high-ranking group of disloyal and incompetent officials were responsible for the approaching triumph of communism in China.

Chiang's influential friend, Henry Luce, turned *Life* magazine into a virtual advertisement for the Kuomintang. In October 1947, shortly after the Administration's critics charged that a high-level report supposedly urging increased military aid for China had been covered up, *Life* carried a sensationalist article by former ambassador to Russia, Roosevelt crony and gadfly, William Bullitt. The real question, Bullitt insisted, was whether China could "be kept out of the hands of Stalin." His answer was not surprising: "Certainly—and at a cost to ourselves which will be small compared to the magnitude of our vital interests in the independence of China."

Like most of Chiang's supporters, Bullitt never explained why America's stake in China was so "vital." The point seemed to be that keeping each and every nation out of communism's control was vital to American security. Bullitt charged that Roosevelt had betrayed China at Yalta through some sort of conspiracy. To make amends and save Asia, he argued, the United States must now spend a fortune, committing itself fully to Chiang's regime.

Bullitt proposed that over the next three years the United States invest over a billion dollars in the Chinese economy, send military and civilian advisors to supervise reforms, and assign General Douglas MacArthur as "Personal Representative of the President" in China to undertake a plan to "prevent subjugation of China by the Soviet Union." Solemnly, Bullitt warned that:

> If China falls into the hands of Stalin, all Asia, including Japan, sooner or later will fall into his hands. The manpower and resources of Asia will be mobilized against us. The independence of the U.S. will not live a generation longer than the independence of China.

Life magazine, it appeared, would rush in where American troops feared to tread. In July 1949 it ran a big spread on General Claire Chennault's efforts to convince Congress to revive the "Flying Tigers" as a "volunteer" combat air force to save Chiang. *Life* called the proposal the "Last Call for China," explaining that Chennault planned to hold a zone in south China. "A Fighting American says that a Third of its Good Earth and 150,000,000 People Can Be Saved." In October 1949 *Reader's Digest* printed an abridged version of this plan with the graphic title, "Hold 'Em! Harrass 'Em! Hamstring 'Em!"

Despite these hysterical warnings by Chiang's friends, the Truman Administration avoided any headlong plunge into the vortex of China's civil war. More responsible political leaders, however great their dislike of Chinese communism, simply did not believe that the United States could "save" the Kuomintang. Truman later remarked that the Chiangs, Kungs and Soongs "were all thieves, every last one of them." Republican Senator Arthur Vandenberg and Democrat Tom Connally, the two leading foreign policy "experts" in the Senate, seemed to agree. Vandenberg, who did not oppose the principle of aiding the Nationalists, admitted in 1948 that "there are limits to our resources and boundaries to our miracles." A year later he remarked that in China "we are facing the conundrum of the ages." Connally spoke more directly: Any more aid to Chiang would be "money down a rat hole." Squandering American resources on a lost bat-

tle seemed idiotic. Instead, the Administration pushed Congress
to build up an anticommunist barrier in Europe where America
could rely on reasonably competent and powerful allies. Still,
pressures brought by the China Lobby and Chiang's die-hard
supporters forced the Truman Administration to approve the
China Aid Act of 1948 which allocated $125 million for use "at
the discretion of the Chinese government."

The policy of the Truman Administration towards the Chinese
civil war was affected not only by personal views of the KMT or
changes in the battlefield situation. Of particular importance
were evaluations coming from the State Department. Policy
planning, especially as influenced by George Kennan during
1948–49, downplayed the overall importance of China. Kennan,
in particular, believed that in terms of U.S. interests in East Asia,
Japan was far more important than China. The U.S., he argued,
ought to concentrate its efforts on rehabilitating Japan and the
Philippines as pro-American bulwarks against Soviet expansion.
Whether or not the CCP or KMT won in China, Kennan proposed, it would neither threaten American security, nor help
the U.S. to contain the U.S.S.R. In his view the Asian mainland
was a backwater to the Cold War whose center remained in
Europe.

Kennan, who typified the "Europe-oriented" policy planner,
lobbied intensively within the Administration against any increase in U.S. involvement in China's civil war. Though he accepted the current belief that the Chinese Communists were
more or less in thrall to the Kremlin, Kennan imagined a possibility that "nationalistic" elements in the CCP might limit Soviet influence. This meant that Washington should be tactically
flexible in dealing with any future Communist regime in China.
During 1948–49, Kennan and his circle in the State Department
continually opposed recommendations from the Defense Department. The military wing of the foreign policy establishment
voiced a keen desire to expand military and economic aid to the
KMT. Already, this group saw the Chinese Communists as a direct threat to American security.

All theories aside, battlefield realities by the end of 1948 cer-
tified the imminent demise of the Kuomintang government. The
Communists had already won control over half the country, the

economy had all but collapsed, and Nationalist troops were defecting to the Reds en masse. Yet, Secretary of State Marshall and the President still refused to clarify the situation to the American people. Marshall told Truman that to do so publicly would "deliver the knock-out blow to the Nationalist government." It was better, he said, to keep the "facts from the American people and thereby not be accused later of playing into the hands of the Communists." Ignorant of the facts (or not caring), in February 1949 fifty senators asked Truman to approve a $1.5 billion loan to the crumbling regime. After the Administration reported that American weapons were being captured by the Communists almost as soon as they reach China, Congress dropped the request to a mere $75 million.

Finally, after three years of avoiding the facts, Truman approved the State Department's preparation of an official explanation of the China debacle. Released in August 1949, the "China White Paper" was a massive review of Chinese-American relations during the previous decade. Intended to deflate Chiang's supporters, the document chronicled KMT decadence, incompetence and corruption. The United States, it concluded, had done all that was possible; Chiang had brought defeat upon himself. The official report never addressed the question of why the American government had done so much to save such a despot.

Hoping to appease conservatives and counter any claim that the White Paper "stabbed Chiang in the back," Secretary of State Dean Acheson appended a "cover letter" to the report which contradicted much of what it contained. In his letter, Acheson declared that the Chinese Communists were abominable villains who had "foresworn their Chinese heritage and have publicly announced their subservience to a foreign power, Russia. . . ." This was what the Administration's critics had claimed all along.

Acheson's charges seemed, in part, to be the American reaction to Mao's June 1949 statement that the Chinese would "lean to one side," supporting the forces of "socialism" against those of "imperialism." This appeared to be a declaration of total hostility towards America. Years later it became known that in private the Communists, including Chou En-lai, had again made several efforts to begin discussions on possibly improving relations with the U.S. Mao and Chou indicated they wished to keep their political and economic options open and thus avoid total dependence on the Soviet Union. While Mao effusively praised the Russians, he implied that China would become an alternative center of power and influence in the Communist world. Although diplomatic planners such as George Kennan had already urged Washington to respond flexibly to such hints of Chinese independence, Secretary of State Dean Acheson took an opposite approach to the issue. He strictly forbade American diplomats in China to respond to Communist feelers. Acheson accepted Mao's public attacks on the U.S. (which in part, at least, were for home consumption and designed to please the Soviets) as proof of the Communists' implacable hostility.

Not surprisingly, Mao responded to these rebuffs by writing several well-publicized essays in 1949 that denounced American policy as a fraud. He urged all Americans and Chinese to read the White Paper and then decide who was a hypocrite. By October 1, 1949, when Mao stood at T'ien An Men to proclaim the People's Republic, the pattern of Sino-American hostility had become fixed. Washington and Peking were bitter enemies. Within a year their armies would be at war in Korea.

Selected Additional Readings

For a discussion of U.S. relations with the CCP during WWII see: Schaller, *The United States Crusade in China,* cited earlier; John S. Service, *Lost Chance in China: The World War II Dispatches of John S. Service,* New York: Random House, 1974; John S. Service, *The Amerasia Papers: Some Problems in the History of U.S.-China Relations,* Berkeley: Center for Chinese Studies, University of California, 1971; John Patton Davies, *Dragon by the Tail,* New York: Norton, 1972.

The politics of the Atomic Bomb are analyzed in Martin J. Sherwin, *A World Destroyed: The Atomic Bomb and the Grand Alliance,* New York: Knopf, 1975.

U.S.-Soviet relations and their effect upon China are discussed in Daniel Yergin, *Shattered Peace: The Origins of the Cold War and the National Security State,* Boston: Houghton Mifflin, 1977.

An eyewitness account of American policy in China during the

Civil War is provided by John Melby, *The Mandate of Heaven: Record of a Civil War, China 1945–1949*, Toronto: University of Toronto Press, 1968.

China's internal politics during the Civil War are lucidly described in Suzanne Pepper, *Civil War in China: The Political Struggle, 1945–1949*, Berkeley: University of California Press, 1978. For a moving account of the struggle in a particular Chinese village see William Hinton, *Fanshen: A Documentary of Revolution in a Chinese Village*, New York: Vintage, 1966.

The purge of America's China experts is chronicled in E. J. Kahn, *The China Hands: America's Foreign Service Officers and What Befell Them*, New York: Penguin Books, 1976.

6

The Red and Yellow Perils

The "loss" of China sent tremors throughout the American political landscape. Americans seemed stunned by the reality of a Communist China allied to the Soviet Union. Conditioned to see the Chinese as eager to adopt American culture and religion, people in the United States were shocked by the new regime's rejection of outside guidance. How could the Communists be so ungrateful as to drive out American missionaries, churches and businesses?* What could impel Mao to journey to Moscow and, in February 1950, sign a military alliance and trade agreement with the hated Stalin? To many the answer seemed clear: the nefarious web of communist subversion had trapped China and betrayed its hapless people.

The terms of the American debate over events in China had relatively little to do with China itself. Essentially, they reflected our own fear of people who challenged American values. By 1950 the cold war with communism in Europe had raged for

---

* Not all American missionaries and businesses were immediately expelled. Washington chose to publicize the expulsions and pressured all U.S. nationals to leave China, in order to emphasize communist hostility. Only with the Korean War did the Chinese move against most of the remaining American residents.

four years. The enemy, centered in Moscow, ensnared nations by subversion and treason. No people, Americans of that time believed, would ever choose to accept communism of their own free will. Americans' sense of omnipotence in China was directly challenged by the Communists' success. Failure in such an area of special interest to the U.S. seemed to prove that someone must have betrayed the effort from the inside. For the next twenty years American policy toward Asia sought first to root out this "treason" and then to limit the contagion of what was called "Red China." As the most knowledgeable American China experts were purged from the government, new experts were found who decreed that the United States must become the policeman of Asia.

Strangely enough, in 1950 and for many years thereafter, only a handful of Americans in or out of government questioned whether China was ours to lose. Few inside the Truman Administration and fewer among its conservative critics considered the root causes of the Chinese revolution. Reports of peasant violence against landlords and the expropriation of foreign-owned and church property were interpreted as evidence of communist madness and a portent of what the Chinese would do to the United States if only given a chance. American political and opinion leaders could not or would not see the significance to the Chinese of the destruction of the power of the landholding classes and the abolition of the special privileges granted foreigners. Looked at through the blinders of western liberalism and the ideology of anticommunism, the Chinese Communists' violent rejection of the American model proved the new regime to be a Russian pawn. As such, Communist China must be considered a threat to American security.

Speaking in 1951, Assistant Secretary of State (later Secretary of State under Presidents Kennedy and Johnson) Dean Rusk expressed this underlying view most graphically. He explained China's involvement in the Korean War and the nature of the Peking leadership in this way:

> The peace and security of China are being sacrificed to the ambitions of a Communist conspiracy. China has been driven by foreign masters into an adventure of foreign aggression. . . . The Pei-

ping* regime may be a colonial Russian government. . . . It is not
the government of China. . . . It is not Chinese. . . .

The fixation which Rusk and others voiced was a bizarre dis-
tortion of America's traditional interest in China. Before 1937
the official role of the American government in China was relatively small. Washington used its influence to dissuade Russian
and Japanese meddling in China and pressed the Chinese not to
discriminate against private American activity. The majority of
the Americans involved with China had always been missionaries, merchants and philanthropists. After 1937 President Roosevelt reversed this policy, seeking to transform China into a
great power and postwar partner through American aid and political support to the Kuomintang. By the late 1940s it had become impossible for most Americans to separate their interests
in China from the preservation of Chiang Kai-shek and the con-
tinuation of KMT rule. A China not ruled by Chiang was, *ipso
facto,* not really Chinese. In the mind of the average American
this former ally was not only a great power, but a sort of Frankenstein's monster controlled by an implacably hostile communist
foe. This vision set the stage for East Asia to become a battle-
ground between the United States and China.

During the first few months of the new regime, American policy remained in a period of flux, waiting, in Dean Acheson's
words, "for the dust to settle." The United States refused to establish diplomatic relations with the Communist regime, prefer-
ring to continue the fiction that Chiang's rump faction on the island of Taiwan was China's legal government. But, at the same
time, the United States made no promise to help defend Taiwan
against the expected Communist attack. Apparently, Truman
and Acheson planned to allow the Chinese civil war to end with
no more direct American interference.

This did not mean that the United States expected to play a
minor role in Asia's future. On the contrary, many actions al-

---

* Rusk, in accord with U.S. government policy, refused to call the Communist capital by its original name, Peking, which means "northern capital." Under the KMT, Nanking was made the capital and the old capital
was renamed Peiping, or "northern peace." This American stubbornness,
which continued until the late 1960s, was designed to show that Washington refused to accept the legality of the Communist regime.

ready taken indicated a strengthened American determination
to control Asian development. Since 1947, for example, American occupation policy in Japan, under the guidance of General
MacArthur, had moved increasingly towards restoring Japan's
economic strength and the influence of its more conservative,
pro-American politicians. Initially it had been U.S. policy to
break up the giant Japanese business monopolies ("zaibatsu")
which had been linked to military expansion. By 1948–49 this
policy was shelved. Instead American occupation authorities
emphasized the rebuilding of Japanese defense forces, the curb-
ing of leftwing political and labor groups and other programs to
enhance rapid recovery. Japan, it seemed, would become the
pivot of U.S. influence in Asia, a role originally slated for Nationalist China.

Within months of the Communist victory in China the State
Department and National Security Council began a comprehensive review of American policy in Asia. Secretary of State Acheson made it plain that the review should be premised with the
determination to defend the rest of Asia from succumbing to
communism. On December 30, 1949, President Truman approved a major National Security Council Study (NSC 48–2)
which placed U.S. policy firmly on a course "set to block further
Communist expansion in Asia." The document recommended
that "particular attention should be given to the problem of
French Indochina."* This "problem" would haunt America for
the next twenty-five years. Though the Administration remained
unsure of what to do and where to do it, it was certain that a
military barrier must soon be drawn around the People's Republic of China.

Red Scare at Home

The Truman Administration's effort to explain events and formulate a new policy in East Asia became nearly impossible after
1950. Both Congress and the American public lost faith in "official" explanations. The China debate became the haunt of

---

* A French colony which included Vietnam, Cambodia, and Laos.

wildly irresponsible demagogues both in government and in the press. The issue of China became only a means to an end—gaining political power by stoking fears of treason and conspiracy committed by career officials and the Democratic Party. Many of postwar America's social and political tensions became wrapped up in the debate over the "loss of China."

Vitriolic accusations concerning the betrayal of China had been voiced as early as November 1945 when Ambassador Hurley resigned. Though given attention then and later, the flamboyant ambassador's reckless charges against allegedly disloyal, procommunist subordinates had failed to persuade most people. Still, enough members of Congress and the Senate and some in the press sympathized with Hurley and Chiang so that the claims of treason were revived in several inconclusive Congressional hearings. But the truly massive search for subversion, the great Red Scare called "McCarthyism," only began in earnest after 1950.

By then political paranoia had a much richer soil in which to grow. Communist China was a reality. Mao had gone to Moscow and signed an alliance with the Soviet Union. One hundred miles off the Chinese mainland lay a vulnerable anticommunist Taiwan, expecting an imminent invasion. In the autumn of 1949 the Russians had ended the American atomic monopoly by exploding an atomic bomb. Within the United States a series of sensational Congressional investigations had attempted to spotlight communist spies in the federal government. Most notably, Congressman Richard Nixon's House Committee on Un-American Activities had "exposed" former State Department official Alger Hiss as a Russian spy. Though the evidence of Hiss's guilt was far from clear, he was finally convicted of perjury (*not* espionage) after a second trial in January 1950.

But spy-mania and fears of treason were not solely the product of professional bigots and red-baiters. The Truman Administration itself had inadvertently contributed to the Red Scare. In 1947, partly to stifle critics, Truman ordered the creation of a federal loyalty program designed to root out any actual spies or potential security risks working for the federal government. During the next five years almost seven million people underwent security investigations. Although not a single person was charged with any illegal act, the investigation itself fueled fears of subversion.

The government's reaction to the detonation of a Russian atomic bomb demonstrated how Washington promoted sensational fears. While Soviet espionage had certainly penetrated the British and American atomic energy research programs, the development of a Soviet A-bomb was an inevitable fact, only marginally speeded up by stealing secrets. Nevertheless, the American government, and especially the FBI, emphasized the espionage angle and carried on a massive search for atomic spies. During the summer of 1950, almost simultaneous with the outbreak of fighting in Korea, the FBI announced the arrest of Julius and Ethel Rosenberg for allegedly passing atomic secrets to the Russians. The confusing legal battle dragged on for three years before the Rosenbergs were executed. Throughout their trial the prosecution and judge made references to how their "treason" had emboldened the Russian and Chinese Communists against America.

In this atmosphere of grave suspicion, witch-hunters found it relatively easy to turn public attention again towards the branch of the State Department which, they claimed, bore responsibility for the "loss of China." The Far Eastern Division was a small, close-knit and highly respected group of career officials. The China area officers, trained during WWII, were considered among the most tested young diplomats in government service. Their reports from wartime China—the warnings about the KMT's fatal flaws, the analyses of Communist power, the recommendations that the U.S. might support the CCP—still stand the test of time for their uncanny accuracy. Ironically, as we have shown, their reports generally had little influence on the major decisions of the Roosevelt and Truman administrations. But during the war years and on into the cold war these Foreign Service officers were resented for committing a grave human error. They continually transmitted unpleasant news to their political superiors. Time and time again their reports from China spoke of KMT corruption and oppression. They predicted the Communists' eventual victory—which in the popular mind became synonymous with being procommunist and causing Chiang's defeat.

One demogogue, in particular, rode the anticommunist fury to fame and power. Among the many witch-hunters in national politics, Wisconsin Senator Joseph McCarthy led the campaign to hunt down traitors. From 1950 to 1954 he and his cohorts terrorized and gutted the Foreign Service, driving respected officials out of office and draping a pall over U.S.-China relations which lasted until 1971. McCarthy claimed a desire to expose and destroy

> individuals who are loyal to the ideal and designs of Communism rather than those of the free, God-fearing half of the world. . . . I refer to the Far Eastern Division of the State Department and the Voice of America.

In reality, this cruel and reckless politician used the largely bogus issue of communists in government to gain fame, notoriety and reelection.

On February 9, 1950, McCarthy "went public" with his accusations. In a speech in Wheeling, West Virginia, he revealed his charges of a massive conspiracy.

> I have here in my hand a list of two hundred and five [names of people] known to the Secretary of State as being members of the Communist Party and who nevertheless are still working and shaping the policy of the State Department.

McCarthy never actually revealed the names of anyone in any way connected with the Communist Party and the State Department. What he did do was to charge that the Foreign Service officers who had so accurately criticized Chiang and predicted his downfall were agents of a "communist conspiracy." He eventually even claimed that Owen Lattimore, a professor of Asian history at Johns Hopkins University, was the "number one Soviet agent" in America.

No one named had been guilty of anything except telling the unpleasant truth. Yet, in this hysterical, anticommunist atmosphere, being accused was tantamount to guilt. Neither Truman nor Eisenhower spoke up to defend the accused diplomats. One by one, during the early 1950s, officers in the China service were driven from their posts as "loyalty" or "security" risks. None was actually charged with willful crime, but with committing absurd indiscretions. For example, Foreign Service personnel who had been stationed with the Dixie Mission in Yenan were criticized for "consorting" with known Communists! By the time President Dwight Eisenhower assumed office, John Carter Vincent, Oliver Clubb, John Davies and John Service had already been or would soon be driven out of the State Department. Some other lesser known diplomats were permitted to stay on provided that they switch areas and stay clear of Chinese affairs. By 1954 virtually no one with expert training or experience in China remained in the Far Eastern Division of the State Department.

Talented junior officials quickly learned to avoid specializing in Chinese affairs because the area was a political mine field. As a result of McCarthyite attacks and the refusal of Presidents Truman and Eisenhower to resist them, an entire generation of government China experts was professionally destroyed. The purge of these diplomats in the prime of their careers ensured that a long time would elapse before the next generation of China specialists emerged. Until then the blind would lead the blind. In a remarkable irony, the United States was ostracizing Americans who had contacts with the Chinese Communists just as the Chinese Communists were punishing their own citizens whom they considered too close to American culture.

The American political inquisition made it both difficult and dangerous for anyone to question the "truth" that China was a vicious enemy—a victim and a tool of world communism. The simplistic division of the world into two camps was not limited to the radical Right. In January 1950 President Truman ordered the National Security Council to review overall American defense policy. The study, named NSC–68 when completed in June, predicted a long-term confrontation between the "free world" (led by the U.S.) and the communist camp (led by the U.S.S.R.). This top secret report (not released until the 1970s) implied a need to increase U.S. defense spending by 300 to 400 percent to confront not only direct Soviet challenges but indigenous nationalist movements attacking colonial or neo-colonial regimes.

NSC–68 served as a "call to arms," a rallying cry for the U.S. and its allies to drastically increase their own military preparedness to resist a perceived Soviet threat. The special State and

Senator Joseph McCarthy smiles after having accused Foreign Service officer John Service of "losing China." (June 1950) (National Archives)

Defense department study group headed by Paul Nitze which prepared the documents described a world in which a communist victory anywhere meant an equivalent loss for the United States. NCS–68 disallowed any gray areas. It hardly distinguished between Soviet expansion, national communist movements, or insurgents fighting in strictly local conflicts. Because U.S. planners now viewed virtually all threats to the status quo as a prelude to Soviet expansion, Americans had a vital stake in intervening to preserve the existing order everywhere.

The Truman Administration hesitated to proclaim this doctrine of American globalism upon its completion. Congress was expected to balk at the huge outlays for weapons it entailed. Administration supporters believed that only a crisis might persuade Congress and the public to support such a radical increase in the military budget. Truman did not formally approve the plan until September 1950. As one of Truman's advisor's put it later: In June 1950 "we were sweating over it and then—with regard to NCS–68—thank God Korea came along."

The Korean War

The outbreak of war in Korea on June 25, 1950, began an escalation of hostility which not only brought about an immediate Sino-American confrontation but eventually led to the war in Vietnam. At the end of World War II, Korea, like Germany (and Vietnam in 1954) was divided by a temporary cease-fire line. Initially, neither the U.S. nor the Soviet Union (the two occupying powers) envisioned a permanent division. However, the growing tensions of the cold war led to the creation of opposing regimes in North and South Korea acting as client states of the two superpowers. By 1949 the Soviets and Americans had built up armies and governments in the two Koreas, led by Kim Il Sung and Syngman Rhee, respectively. After this, foreign occupation forces withdrew.

Historians now generally agree that China was not directly involved in planning the North Korean attack on the south. The fledgling regime in Peking was still preparing to fight Chiang's remnants on Taiwan. Stalin, however, must have given at least tacit approval to the attack. While the North Korean aim was to unify the country (a goal shared with equal fervor by Syngman Rhee), the Soviets may have also hoped that a quick victory over South Korea would dissuade Japan from joining the United States in a military and political alliance. In any case, there had been sporadic border incidents between the two Koreas for some time and no one expected that the United States would involve itself in a large-scale war over Korea. During early 1950 Secretary of State Acheson had even omitted Korea from his description of the American "defense perimeter" in Asia.

The actual American response to word of the North Korean

attack was far more sweeping than anyone outside the Truman Administration might have guessed. On June 27, 1950, Truman declared that the "attack upon Korea makes it plain beyond all doubt that Communism had passed beyond the use of subversion to conquer independent nations and will now use armed invasion and war."

The President quickly ordered both a general build-up of American military strength and American assistance to the retreating South Korean forces. Under the mantle of a U.N. resolution (passed only because the Soviet delegate boycotted meetigns of the Security Council to protest the U.N.'s failure to seat the Peking government), American ground, sea and air forces rushed into Korea after June 27.

The most significant and ultimately disastrous aspect of the American response to the North Korean attack was the decision to draw a military barrier around Communist China and become reinvolved in the civil war. American officials argued that the fighting in Korea was not a local phenomenon, but rather the first probe in a communist master plan to control all Asia and Europe. Suddenly, American leaders possessed a rationale to create anticommunist bulwarks around China. Not only would South Korea be defended, but now Taiwan would be shielded from invasion. After declaring that "the occupation of Formosa by Communist forces would be a direct threat to the security of the Pacific area . . . ," Truman ordered the U.S. 7th Fleet to take up a position in the Taiwan Straits in order to prevent an invasion of Chiang's island bastion.

Simultaneous with this decision, Washington announced that aid to the French colonial forces in Indochina would be dramatically increased. Ho Chi Minh, leader of the Vietminh guerrillas against the French, was adjudged to be nothing more than another puppet of the communist conspiracy. American military and economic aid would be supplied to preserve a pro-Western anticommunist regime on China's periphery. By 1954, the United States was paying eighty percent of the cost of the French war and had already dispatched its own "advisory" mission to Saigon.

From Peking's perspective, these American actions critically threatened China's security. Whatever the Chinese Communists may have felt about the Korean fighting, they were obviously

worried about how American activity there might endanger
China. By intervening in Korea, the United States had apparently resumed its defense of Chiang, making an immediate
invasion of Taiwan impossible. Washington had also declared its
intention of supporting unfriendly regimes around China, such
as in French Indochina. On June 28, Communist spokesman
Chou En-lai declared that American actions in Korea and Taiwan constituted "aggression against the territory of China.
. . . It is precisely a further act of intervention by American
imperialism in the affairs of Asia." As Peking saw it, the United
States had begun to encircle China militarily and was renewing
its support for the Kuomintang regime on Taiwan.

United States' conduct of the war from June through Novem-
ber, 1950, only heightened China's fears. General Douglas Mac-
Arthur, who commanded American forces, did almost everything
imaginable to identify U.S. action in Korea as aimed against
China. In Taiwan he ostentatiously conferred with Chiang Kai-
shek, then leaked his opinion that KMT troops should be used
in the war. Furthermore, when American forces landed at
Inchon, South Korea in September 1950, MacArthur pressed
Washington for authority to carry the war into North Korea, to
China's doorstep.

After driving the North Koreans out of the South, MacArthur
convinced the administration to permit him to cross the old
border at the 38th parallel and destroy the North Korean regime.
Once this was done, the U.S. and U.N. would presumably create
an united, anticommunist Korea. Since MacArthur's initial military moves were so successful, both the Truman Administration
and U.N. proved willing to go along with his strategy.

The decision to destroy the North Korean government created
an entirely new war. Unfortunately the United States political
leadership ignored the possible Chinese Communist reaction to
the specter of the fanatically anticommunist MacArthur leading
an American army right to the Korean-Chinese border. Given
MacArthur's past actions and statements it was not unlikely that
he might stage an incident to provoke a war between China and
the U.S. However, during September and October, MacArthur's
rapid military victories covered up these concerns. The Truman

Administration, moreover, did not want to appear to be stifling its most gallant and successful general, a hero who was "rolling back the iron curtain."

The Chinese could not afford to remain silent at the prospect of MacArthur approaching the Yalu River, where Manchuria—China's industrial heartland—and Korea met. To permit an American army and, perhaps, eventually KMT troops to approach this region was unthinkable. Even if these forces did not attack China proper, how could Peking permit the U.S. to create a new anticommunist Korea without courting grave future dangers? Finally, no one in Peking (or Washington) could be sure that MacArthur would follow Washington's orders that China not be attacked. Once American forces entered China, withdrawal would be nearly impossible.

Hoping to prevent a wider war, the Peking leadership tried to convince Washington to restrain MacArthur. Chou En-lai sent numerous public and private messages to the U.S. stating that China could not and would not "stand idly by" if American forces crossed the 38th parallel and tried to destroy North Korea. Even though its existence was officially denied by the U.N., the Peking government planned to send a special delegate to that world body to explain its policy.

Apparently, China's warnings were outweighed by the optimism resulting from MacArthur's initial military success. Here, after five frustrating years of cold war, was an American general defeating communists on a real battlefield. To most Americans it did not really matter which communists were being killed or whether China was really the country responsible for the fighting in Korea. As long as MacArthur's actions were successful, the Truman Administration would piggyback along for the credit, ignoring China's warnings.

At a deeper level, however, Truman and Secretary of State Acheson profoundly disagreed with General MacArthur. MacArthur advocated what amounted to an immediate all out war against communism beginning with China. The Truman Administration insisted that the balance of power in the world remained in Europe and that the U.S. could not afford to engage in peripheral wars given the limitations of its military forces.

The Administration did intend to "take advantage" of Korea in the sense that the war justified a huge American military build up as outlined in NSC–68. Military spending increased from about $13 billion to $50 billion in three years. Much of the build-up actually took place in Europe rather than in Korea.

Aside from this strategic debate, Truman and his aides were continually outraged by MacArthur's freewheeling political and military policies. The general made shameless use of press leaks and private talks with politicians, as well as undertaking unauthorized military acts to push administration policy along lines acceptable to him. MacArthur frequently disobeyed or circumvented direct orders he found distasteful. In October a nervous Truman flew to Wake Island to consult with his General (who did not deign to fly to Washington) and received a condescending assurance that the war was virtually won and that the danger of Chinese intervention was minimal.

The bubble burst in November 1950 as American troops approached the Chinese border. The United States had ignored Peking's many alarms and MacArthur dismissed mounting intelligence reports that Chinese troops were already in position to resist American forces. Not even several brief engagements with Chinese troops gave MacArthur pause. Instead, the bellicose general announced an "end the war" offensive. The authoritative Peking *People's Daily* of November 11 expressed in words what was happening already on the battlefield. Chinese "volunteers" were counterattacking the American army because this was the only way to prevent an invasion of China. Peking insisted it had no remaining options. China must "Check them with force and compel them to stop . . . there is no alternative." Caught totally unprepared by this counterattack, the American army was swept south in the longest retreat in United States military history. Over the next three years, the war caused 142,000 American and almost one million Chinese casualties. Among those killed in the fighting was Mao Tse-tung's son.

Only five years earlier Chinese armies had been allies against Japan. Now "Red Chinese hordes" (in the current phrase) were slaughtering Americans. MacArthur and the American press reacted as if Chinese intervention was totally unexpected and unjustified. As one contemporary war newsreel reported:

Americans were being routed by Chinese Red Army legions, treacherously forced into this war by the unscrupulous leaders of international communism . . . as the G.I.'s battle the new elements with everything they have, but the latest Communist perfidy in Korea makes the picture grim.

The "new war" in Korea presented a terrible dilemma to the American government. Truman's advisors feared that too wide a war with China in Korea would weaken resistance to possible Soviet expansion in Europe or bring Soviet forces into China itself. MacArthur and his right-wing supporters, fixated on the dangers of Chinese Communism, campaigned for a massive counterattack upon China. They bitterly opposed Truman's decision to contain the fight in Korea while expanding military strength in Europe. Unable to convince his superiors to expand the war into China, MacArthur began to appeal directly to the American people and leaders of the Republican opposition through speeches and news leaks. Such behavior made the Chinese even more frightened, since it was increasingly unclear who actually spoke for the United States, Truman or MacArthur.

Yet Truman did not dismiss MacArthur from his command until the spring of 1951, by which time the war in Korea had become a stationary affair. The Chinese were convinced that American intervention was really aimed at them, while most Americans were certain that Chinese intervention was part of an orchestrated plot. The war dragged on until March 1953 when an armistice virtually reestablished the prewar borders. But by then the United States had already committed itself to a vast new undertaking in Asia—the permanent military and political containment of Communist China.

The Republicans Take Command

The stalemated war in Korea further discredited a president and Democratic Party already charged with disloyalty and corruption. During the 1952 presidential campaign enterprising Republicans popularized a slogan, "K^1C^2," signifying Democratic responsibility for "Korea, Communism and Corruption." Even more striking was the phrase coined by Senator Joe McCarthy:

Since 1933, he intoned, the Democrats had perpetrated "Twenty Years of Treason."

Promising to end the stalemate in Korea and fight the "international communist conspiracy" more vigorously, Republicans Dwight D. Eisenhower and Senator Richard M. Nixon, the Vice-Presidential nominee, rode a tide of victory into the White House. The 1952 campaign was clear warning to American politicians—anyone tainted with the "loss" of a country to communism faced near certain electoral defeat. No one, Republican or Democrat, could risk the charge of compromising with the devil or being "soft." Thereafter, American policy, especially in Asia, became largely a knee-jerk reaction. Any regime, no matter how corrupt or reactionary, could call on American assistance if it was threatened by a revolutionary movement and the Americans would feel required to respond.

This rigid political stance was encouraged by the activities of the China Lobby in the United States. Dedicated to aiding Taiwan and opposing the People's Republic, the China Lobby emerged as an informal watchdog over American foreign policy. The largest and most influential of these groups was the "Committee of One Million," established in 1953 to resist any tendency towards improvement of U.S.-Chinese Communist relations. The China Lobby was particularly influential in Congress, continually pushing that body toward extreme anti-Chinese Communist position. Any politician who suggested a more moderate policy risked incurring the organized wrath of the China Lobby. The group directed its influence and funds on behalf of "friends" and against "enemies." This pressure was often successful.

It is inaccurate to assume, however, that American policy towards Communist China was manipulated solely by lobbyists for Taiwan. A broad range of American political, military, economic, religious and intellectual leaders was convinced that the P.R.C. represented a real danger to the security of the United States. Since these leaders were certain China was actively spreading revolution in Asia, American policy after 1950 centered on the creation of anticommunist bulwarks surrounding China.

The Eisenhower Administration placed the final bricks in the wall around China begun by the Truman Administration. In 1953 Eisenhower appointed John Foster Dulles as Secretary of State. An accomplished international lawyer and elder of the Presbyterian Church, Dulles brought a special moralism to his China policy. The new Secretary, who enjoyed Eisenhower's trust, had observed the power of the anticommunist zealots in Congress to hamstring the previous administration. Partly to avoid criticism from that contingent, Dulles exhibited the behavior and rhetoric most likely to placate the McCarthyites. He accepted their allegations that disloyal diplomats had subverted American policy in China and announced that, henceforth, mere loyalty to U.S. policy was insufficient: diplomats would have to demonstrate "positive loyalty"—whatever that meant. One thing it did mean was that the few remaining China experts in the State Department, who had been critical of Chiang, such as John Carter Vincent, were forced to resign. Furthermore, Dulles appointed a special assistant, Scott McLeod, whose duty it was to oversee the Foreign Service and root out "subversives."

Dulles's view of China throughout the 1950s was similar to that expressed by Rusk in 1951. Between Republicans and Democrats after the outbreak of the Korean War there was little difference over China. As one of his aides put it, Dulles continued to dream "his fancy about reactivating the civil war in China." He deeply believed the People's Republic of China was a "godless," illegal regime which did not "conform to the practices of civilized nations." The U.S., he insisted, must never recognize or do business with Peking. Instead, it must promote conditions leading to the overthrow of the regime. In 1957 Dulles declared, "We owe it to ourselves, our allies, and the Chinese people to do all that we can to contribute to that passing."

The compromise which ended the Korean War in 1953 (though American combat troops remained in the South) was a policy of expedience, and did not signal acceptance of the Peking regime. Both before and after the Korean armistice, Washington maneuvered to contain China. At the close of 1951 the United States ended the formal occupation of Japan. John Foster Dulles, then serving as special advisor to the Truman Administration, had drafted a mutual security treaty with Tokyo that linked the two nations in a military pact aimed against China and the Soviet Union. The Japanese promised to recognize Chiang's regime on Taiwan as the legitimate Chinese government and permitted American military forces to remain in Japan.

After the end of fighting in Korea, the Eisenhower Administration continued to oppose any relaxation of tensions with China. On the contrary, new and larger schemes for containment were devised. In September 1954 Dulles fathered the Southeast Asia Treaty Organization (SEATO). SEATO was a bloc of anticommunist states on China's periphery which were organized under American sponsorship into a regional defense alliance. In December 1954 the United States and Taiwan entered a mutual defense treaty which pledged American support for Taiwan against any threat from China. American military and intelligence forces utilized Taiwan as a base of operations from the 1950s through the mid-1970s.

In addition to these physical barriers, the Eisenhower Administration maintained a strategic trade embargo on economic contacts with China. Neither Americans nor Europeans nor Japanese who did business with the United States, were permitted to trade in a wide variety of products and technology with China. The trade embargo, Washington hoped, would weaken China's economic and military structure, hastening the collapse of the Communist regime.

The American blockade extended to human beings as well as equipment. During the 1940s several thousand Chinese students and scientists had come to America for study and training. Now many wished to return home, but to China, not Taiwan. The United States government refused to permit their return until the mid-1950s. Lest the American people be duped by communist propaganda, Secretary of State Dulles forbade American journalists from accepting repeated invitations to visit China. He also barred Chinese journalists from visiting the United States.

While many American acts were more spiteful than dangerous, U.S. policy included several more aggressive activities. During the 1950s and 1960s, Washington sponsored a limited secret war against China, largely under CIA control. Beginning as early as the Korean War, the CIA cooperated with the Nationalists on Taiwan in staging frequent raids on the mainland. These included assaults across the Taiwan Straits, attacks from the Nationalist-held offshore islands (some only 2 miles from the coast), military overflights, and border raids staged by KMT armies which had retreated from China into Burma in 1949.* One of the more bizarre projects carried on during the 1950s was a CIA operation organized in Colorado. There, Tibetan guerrillas were trained in mountain warfare for later airdropping into Tibet. Supposedly, these special forces would lead an uprising against Peking's rule in that part of China. At the time, rumors of such activities were brushed off by U.S. officials as "Communist propaganda." Most of these military operations were of little more than nuisance value, although they did indicate where America stood. The real danger to the Peking regime arose more from the fact that throughout the 1950s Chiang continued to proclaim his intention of "recapturing the mainland." Since, by the terms of the 1954 treaty, Washington was formally allied to Chiang, the Chinese Communists had to assume that the United States might sometime support a full-scale KMT invasion. Even though American leaders privately informed Chiang not to expect American military backing for an invasion of the mainland, the Communists saw the CIA's limited secret war as evidence to the contrary.

Considering the wide scope of American hostility—military provocations, aid to and protection of Taiwan, military support for anticommunist regimes bordering China—it is not hard to understand China's intense hostility towards the United States. From Peking's perspective, it was encircled and continually threatened by American power. As most Americans saw it, Peking was the threat: U.S. policy was merely the sensible response. It was true, for example, that Peking continually denounced the United States once the Korean War began. The Chinese people were encouraged to "hate" America as an ag-

* The KMT forces in the "Golden Triangle" of Burma, Thailand and Laos supplemented their anticommunist activities by becoming major producers of opium and heroin for sale in the U.S. and elsewhere. The CIA-controlled airline which assisted them, Air America, was often called "Air Opium."

gressive imperialist nation. Chinese leaders proclaimed support for revolutionary struggles around the world. "American Imperialism" was considered China's greatest enemy.

In fact, however, China's external behavior was almost always more moderate than its rhetoric championing revolution. Despite China's claims and America's fears, China remained an underdeveloped society. Communist China, throughout the 1950s, was struggling to recover from a half century of political, military, and economic chaos. Its leaders were attempting to reshape their society fundamentally, creating a new agricultural and industrial order. The task was both enormous and costly. Age-old traditions of elitism and superstition had to be overcome, often by harsh regimentation. Peasant hatred against former landlords was a useful tool which the Communist Party could use to mobilize the apolitical and long-suppressed peasants. At times, the outpouring of long-suffered fury led to the slaughter of landlords before the government called a halt to village trials. In an effort to shake off the legacy of imperialism, the new regime threw out most foreigners and missionaries, closing their schools, churches and businesses. These acts, plus China's support for the Soviet Union, convinced Americans that China was led by villains and madmen. In their concern, Americans lost sight of the fact that China's massive effort to overcome backwardness left few resources available for international mischief. While China might cheer on other people's efforts at national liberation, she could do little more than give advice.

Chinese foreign policy since the creation of the People's Republic has had two sides. On the one hand, Mao proclaimed the doctrine that all reactionary and imperialist regimes were "paper tigers," doomed to eventual destruction. Simultaneously, however, the Chinese Communists recognized the existing superior military power of the United States and its allies. Thus, the Chinese emphasized the need for the colonial and exploited peoples of Asia to accomplish their own liberation, without depending on outside help. China would resort to arms only in self-defense, to protect its own territory or to protect friendly regimes on its borders.

Unlike American foreign policy after the Korean War, the

Chinese did not adopt an inflexible and dogmatic approach to the West. While Washington sought to isolate and hoped to topple the Peking regime, the Communists retained some interest in an accommodation. During 1954–55, Chinese Premier and Foreign Minister Chou En-lai once again invited the United States to begin direct talks aimed at improving relations.* Dulles ignored Chou's approach, denying the possibility that one might negotiate with such an evil regime. This uncompromising policy was reflected by the anticommunist zealot, Karl Rankin, sent by Dulles as ambassador to Taiwan. There could be no peace in Asia, Rankin declared, until the "predatory regime" which had stolen China under the "flag of a Communist conspiracy" was replaced by a real Chinese government. By this he meant the. return of all China to Chiang Kai-shek's rule. This outlook propelled the United States into a series of military confrontations with China during the 1950s and 1960s.

In 1955 and especially in 1958 the United States and China came close to war over a crisis in the Taiwan Straits. The Nationalists had retained control over several offshore islands, the most important of which, Quemoy and Matsu, lay only a few miles from the mainland. The large KMT garrisons stationed on the islands were a constant provocation and the islands themselves were used to stage commando attacks upon the mainland.† In an apparent effort to compel a KMT withdrawal—which would eliminate a military threat, mobilize Chinese morale and, it was hoped, weaken resolve on Taiwan—the Communists began to blockade and shell Quemoy in August 1958. Peking, which declared the islands to be Chinese territory, may have also been testing how far the United States would go in defense of Taiwan and whether the Soviet Union would honor its alliance with China. Not only did the Soviet Union seem

---

* Speaking both from inside China and while on foreign missions, Chou urged that the American government permit its citizens to visit China and accept the legitimacy of the Peking government. Dulles refused all offers and barred the proposed exchange of visits.
† Although the KMT armies could not hope to reconquer the mainland, they had been lavishly re-armed by the U.S. since the Korean War. This gave them the strength to resist a Communist invasion while harrassing the mainland.

somewhat hesitant to stand fully behind Peking, but the Eisenhower Administration rushed to bolster its support of the Nationalists.

Testifying in secret before the Senate Foreign Relations Committee in January 1955 (during the earlier crisis), Dulles stated that the U.S. did not intend to use its own might to restore Chiang's rule over China. Washington had also received a private assurance from the KMT leader that he would not attack the mainland without U.S. permission. At the same time the Secretary of State explained that the U.S. would be prepared to launch air and sea strikes against Communist forces on the mainland that posed a threat to Taiwan.

> We have got to be prepared to take a risk of war with China if we are going to stay in the Far East. . . . If we are not willing to take that risk, all right, let's make that decision and we get out and we make our defense in California.

Congress followed the lead of Dulles and Eisenhower by enacting the Formosa Straits Resolution which empowered the President to use force to protect "the security of Formosa [Taiwan], the Pescadores, and related positions and territories of that area." Dulles even threatened to use atomic bombs against China. He apparently belittled the possibility that Chiang had provoked or exacerbated the crisis in hopes of reinvolving the U.S. in the civil war.

War was avoided during the 1958 crisis by a series of adroit American maneuvers. U.S. Navy ships were employed to run the blockade of the offshore islands, a direct challenge the Chinese were not eager to confront. Once the danger of the island garrisons being starved out had passed, Dulles pressed Chiang to soften his position. During an October visit to Taiwan the Secretary of State apparently warned the Generalissimo against attempting to invade the mainland or expecting American assistance should he do so. But even as this crisis subsided a greater confrontation between the United States and China was brewing in Southeast Asia. It would lead to the longest and most frustrating war in American history.

Selected Additional Readings

E. J. Kahn, *The China Hands*, cited earlier, continues the chronicle of the purge within the Department of State of China policy experts. A personal account of how one diplomat suffered at the hands of the witch-hunters is found in O. Edmund Clubb, *The Witness and I*, New York: Columbia University Press, 1974.

For an intriguing discussion of Republican foreign policy towards China and elsewhere during the Eisenhower Administration see Townsend Hoopes, *The Devil and John Foster Dulles*, Boston: Little, Brown, 1974.

The political activity of the China Lobby is analyzed in Stanley Bachrack, *The Committee of One Million: China Lobby Politics, 1953–1971*, New York: Columbia University Press, 1976.

China's perception of American policy in the early stages of the Korean war is discussed in Allen S. Whiting, *China Crosses the Yalu: The Decision To Enter the Korean War*, New York: Macmillan, 1960.

For a general introduction to the topic of U.S.-Chinese Communist relations during the 1950s and 1960s see Foster Rhea Dulles, *American Foreign Policy Toward Communist China, 1949–1969*, New York: Crowell, 1972.

The unholy alliance of anticommunist politics and the heroin trade is chronicled in Alfred W. McCoy, *The Politics of Heroin in Southeast Asia*, New York: Harper & Row, 1972.

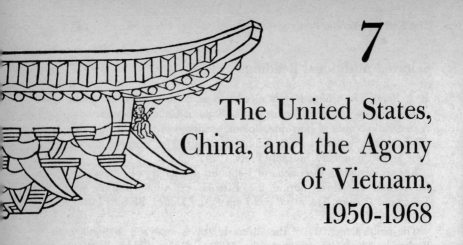

7

The United States, China, and the Agony of Vietnam, 1950-1968

American involvement in Southeast Asia became significant as early as the Korean War. The Truman Administration believed that the Vietnamese nationalists battling the French colonial regime were simply pawns of "the international communist conspiracy" and began to subsidize the cost of the war for the French. As far back as 1945 and 1946, American officials had spurned Ho Chi Minh's request for support in his struggle for independence. Then, as later, Washington refused to accept the possibility that a nationalist movement could be popular and independent while also committed to carry out a radical social revolution. American policymakers remained convinced that the "communist" component of Vietnamese nationalism outweighed any virtues it might possess.

Despite substantial American aid, by 1954 the French were on the verge of defeat. The support of the French people for the conflict had eroded as casualties mounted. In the spring of 1954, the imminent defeat of the French garrison fighting at the battle of Dienbienphu made a quick end to the war likely. Most observers expected that negotiations at the upcoming international conference at Geneva would result in Ho's Viet Minh forces gaining control over all Vietnam.

The Eisenhower Administration, committed to the military and political containment of China, was horrified by the prospect of Vietnam being "lost to communism." Such an event, the Administration feared, would not only weaken "the free world," but would expose the Republicans to Democratic charges that they, too, were "soft on communism." Vice-President Nixon, Secretary of State Dulles, and senior military advisors all urged President Eisenhower to use American air strikes, perhaps even an atomic bomb, against the Viet Minh troops besieging the French at Dienbienphu. While Eisenhower rejected this alternative (the British and French were not enthusiastic), plans went forward to create a new pro-American, anticommunist regime in at least part of Vietnam should the French withdraw.

In May 1954, as the Geneva Conference commenced, the French garrison at Dienbienphu fell and France opted to end the war. Although Dulles briefly attended the Conference (where he refused to speak or to shake hands with Chou En-lai), the Americans declined to sign the Geneva Accords issued in July. These Accords declared that France would leave Indochina (Cambodia, Laos and Vietnam), that Vietnam would be temporarily divided at the 17th parallel to permit the disengagement of forces, and that national elections would be held in 1956 to create a unified nation. In the meantime, no outside powers were to introduce weapons or troops into the area. Dulles agreed informally that the U.S. would abide by the provisions of the Geneva settlement despite his refusal to sign it. For the moment it seemed the best that could be expected. Subsequently the Eisenhower Administration proceeded to violate the Accords repeatedly.

The United States tried to reverse the verdict of the French defeat in Vietnam by accelerating plans to encircle China with a ring of anticommunist, pro-American states. By the close of 1954 Dulles had forged the SEATO alliance and firmed up the U.S. mutual security treaty with Taiwan. Since no friendly, viable regime existed in the southern part of Vietnam (by agreement at Geneva, Ho Chi Minh had already established control north of the 17th parallel demarcation line), American planners resolved to create one before the scheduled national elections in 1956.

During 1954 the CIA and other U.S. personnel were active in Saigon, creating the framework for a government to replace the French. To many Americans, both in and out of government, Vietnam was a special challenge—an opportunity for the United States to create an Asian regime in its own image. Such a scheme had many apparent virtues. Not only would a pro-American regime in Saigon act as a physical barrier to Chinese-Vietnamese Communist expansion, but it would symbolize a successful political alternative to communist revolution in the underdeveloped world. A democratic, prosperous, prowestern and capitalist South Vietnam could be a showcase for U.S. policy in Asia. Probably, American leaders thought of how well they had succeeded in restructuring defeated Japan, so that now its society appeared democratic, pro-western and thoroughly anticommunist. The fundamental social and economic differences between Vietnam and Japan—the former a preindustrial, traditional and rural society, the latter an urbanized, modern industrial state—were subtleties lost on the American mind. American planners thought of Vietnam as clay in their hands, to be molded at will, regardless of what the Vietnamese wanted or the Geneva Accords called for.

The concept of making Vietnam a "showcase" of democracy in Asia also fit neatly into the current theory of global strategy. Beginning under Truman and accelerating under Eisenhower, American policymakers posited a world of political "dominoes." According to this theory, a communist advance in one vulnerable spot would quickly spread and topple over adjacent noncommunist, pro-American governments. Like a row of falling dominoes, the chain reaction was nearly impossible to stop once begun. Thus, holding every piece of noncommunist real estate in Asia became vital to American security since its loss might start the dominoes falling. This mechanistic theory completely ignored the actual sources of instability in most poor Asian countries. Where communist insurgent movements were active, their success or failure was due almost entirely to local support, not Moscow's or Peking's control or aid. Pro-American regimes in Southeast Asia and elsewhere were vulnerable because they were unable or unwilling to rectify fundamental social problems. No amount of U.S. economic or military aid could alter the basically corrupt policies of an unpopular regime. It had not worked in China and would not work elsewhere.

Disregarding history, American leaders believed outside reform could be successful if only the United States would intervene earlier and more completely in Asia to stop the spread of communism. Vietnam had the dubious distinction of being Washington's classroom for a public experiment in counterrevolutionary nation building.

The man the Eisenhower Administration tapped to rule southern Vietnam was, fortuitously, living in the United States. Ngo Dinh Diem came from a prominent Vietnamese Catholic family (the Vietnamese were overwhelmingly Buddhist) and enjoyed support from a number of American academic and political notables, including Senators John Kennedy and Mike Mansfield, Cardinal Spellman and Supreme Court Justice William O. Douglas. A group of political science specialists at Michigan State University (which received a U.S. government contract to help set up a regime in Saigon) championed Diem and helped convince the CIA and other important groups in Washington to support him as the leader of a new Vietnamese government. Diem, it appeared, was a new and improved Chiang Kai-shek—Christian, anticommunist and pro-American.

By the end of 1954 extensive American economic and military support had enabled Diem to establish himself with a personal army in Saigon. By 1956 he had increased his power over a large part of Vietnam south of the 17th parallel. As the scheduled 1956 elections approached, Diem proclaimed the existence of the "Republic of Vietnam" in the south as an independent nation. Washington quickly recognized its own creation and declared that it would defend South Vietnam's "independence and freedom." Since, as Eisenhower admitted in his memoirs, Ho Chi Minh would probably win any free election in Vietnam, neither Washington nor Saigon would permit a vote.

Thus, as of 1956, the U.S. declared there were two separate Vietnams—Ho's "Democratic Republic of Vietnam" in the North and Diem's "Republic of Vietnam" in the South. This arrangement was appalling to most Vietnamese who had no concept of "two Vietnams." The division not only violated the Geneva Accords of 1954 but flew in the face of the prolonged Vietnamese struggle to throw out foreign influence and create an independent, unified nation. Nevertheless, Washington was now committed to preserving Saigon both as a model of nation building and as a barrier to presumed Chinese Communist expansion.

The struggle which soon erupted in southern Vietnam in many ways resembled the earlier war against the French. Guerrilla fighters in the South—the Vietcong—began an insurrection against the Saigon regime. As the rebellion spread, leading to increased repression and foreign (U.S.) intervention, the North came to the aid of their brothers in the South. North Vietnamese troops and large scale aid only appeared later in the conflict, after it had escalated.

Five successive presidential administrations—from Eisenhower through Ford—ignored or denied the nature of the civil war in Vietnam. American leaders—buttressed by fallacious arguments from their national security advisors—insisted that the North Vietnamese and Vietcong were nothing more than proxies fighting against South Vietnam on behalf of China and the Soviet Union. Permitting this aggression to succeed would endanger world peace. To prevent the feared "domino" from falling, the United States committed itself to the defense of South Vietnam.

As a senator in 1956 John Kennedy described Vietnam as the "cornerstone of the Free World in Southeast Asia, the Keystone to the arch, the Finger in the dike." As soon as he became President in 1961, Kennedy's "New Frontier" laid the groundwork for a wider American involvement in Vietnam. Despite his calls to propose new solutions to international problems, Kennedy's foreign policy embraced many existing cold war cliches. While JFK occasionally spoke of the need to improve relations with China, he did not permit members of his administration to pursue innovations. Instead, the major thrust of Kennedy's policies towards the Third World was an effort to expand and perfect "counter-insurgency" warfare. The judicious application of Special Forces (the Green Berets) and CIA covert operations combined with increased military and economic aid to friendly regimes was seen as a way of sweeping back the tide of change in the underdeveloped world. The New Frontier remained convinced that developing societies must follow the American model or else be considered hostile.

Kennedy's policy towards Vietnam was bound to exacerbate the situation and worsen relations with China. JFK chose Dean Rusk as his Secretary of State, a man with a long history of antagonism towards China. Rusk adhered to the belief that it was "as essential to 'contain' communist aggression [in Asia as] in Europe." During his nearly eight years of tenure under Kennedy and Johnson, Rusk frequently raised the specter of "one or two billion Chinese armed with nuclear weapons" as a justification for American involvement in Vietnam. In his mind, Ho Chi Minh and the leaders of the People's Republic of China could only be compared to Adolph Hitler, and their policies to Nazi aggression.

Surrounded by such advisors, prodded by an entrenched anticommunist bureaucracy, and himself ever mindful of Truman's misfortune at being blamed for the "loss of China," Kennedy was determined not to abandon the Saigon regime. By 1962–63 this was a major problem since Diem's position was growing weaker and he was forced to turn more and more to repression of political enemies. While the Vietcong overran large parts of the south, Diem's wrath fell upon the noncommunist opposition to his regime. Like Chiang, Diem seemed to fear his liberal opponents (who might be a magnet for U.S. support) as much as he feared the communists. During the autumn of 1963 Americans were shocked to see on television gruesome films of Buddhist monks immolating themselves in protest against Diem's political and religious oppression. Despite Kennedy's efforts to shore up Saigon by steadily increasing the level of aid and number of U.S. military advisors (from 800 to 16,000), South Vietnam seemed on the verge of collapse. Not only did this threaten a communist advance in Asia, but it loomed as an awesome domestic political setback for the Kennedy Administration. This president had no desire to be called the first president to lose a war—whether or not the charge had any meaning.

To buy some time to shore up South Vietnam, Diem would have to go. The longer this unstable puppet remained in power the more likely the pro-American group in Saigon would lose whatever hold on power it still retained. By the end of October word had filtered down from the White House to South Vietnamese army officers that the U.S. favored the accession of a new regime in Saigon. On November 1, 1963, Diem and his closest aides were slain in a coup, to be succeeded by a line of tin-horn generals. The last of these, Nguyen Van Thieu, would flee to Taiwan in 1975.

Kennedy's own assassination three weeks later brought no reassessment of American policy in Asia. Like his predecessor, Lyndon Johnson was a committed cold warrior and a believer in the theory of falling dominoes. "We will not permit," he declared, "the independent nations of the East to be swallowed by Communist conquest." Nor was LBJ alone in this belief. Richard Nixon, titular leader of the Republican Party, solemnly intoned his belief that "a United States defeat in Vietnam means a Chinese Communist victory."

Johnson, torn between his desire to fund Great Society social programs at home and to defend the faith abroad, fell into the same trap as his predecessors. Reflecting on his decision to escalate the war in 1965, Johnson told his biographer, Doris Kearns,

> if I left that war and let the Communists take over South Vietnam, then I would be seen as a coward and my nation would be seen as an appeaser and we would both find it impossible to accomplish anything for anybody on the entire globe. . . . everything I knew about history told me that if I got out of Vietnam and let Ho Chi Minh run through the streets of Saigon then I'd be doing exactly what Chamberlain did in WWII. I'd be giving a big fat reward to aggression. And I knew that if we let Communist aggression succeed in taking over South Vietnam there would follow in this country an endless national debate—a mean and destructive debate —that would shatter my Presidency, kill my administration and damage our democracy. I knew that Harry Truman and Dean Acheson had lost effectiveness from the day the Communists took over China. I believed that the loss of China had played a large role in the rise of Joe McCarthy. And I knew that all these problems, taken together, were chickenshit compared with what might happen if we lost Vietnam.

Johnson's "theory" about communist aggression and domestic reaction was part self-serving rationalization and part a ménage of misinformation about the nature of the civil war in Vietnam. He cast the giant United States as the victim of a heinous attack by tiny Vietnam. America was the injured party which had no choice but to fight for justice.

This distorted reality became evident in August 1964 during the Tonkin Gulf incident. In a report to Congress, Johnson alleged that U.S. Navy destroyers were attacked by North Vietnamese ships while on peaceful patrol in international waters. Congress responded almost unanimously by passing the "Gulf of Tonkin Resolution," an open-ended statement giving Johnson a free hand to resist attacks on U.S. forces in Southeast Asia. With hardly a perfunctory investigation, Congress approved what amounted to a virtual declaration of war against North Vietnam.

Only several years later did subsequent investigations reveal the administration's duplicity. U.S. naval forces at the time of the Tonkin incident had actually been sailing along a strip of the North Vietnamese coast where American ships had recently assisted South Vietnamese coastal raids. Thus, the attacks were hardly unprovoked. Even more startling, several American sailors testified that no North Vietnamese attack had occurred. They had only detected some unidentified electronic sightings which were erroneously reported as attacks. Again, the specter of revolution abroad and the Red Scare at home pushed American leaders into a reflex decision to fight in Asia.

Following his election in November 1964 (in which he promised *not* to escalate the war), Johnson saw no alternative but to become more involved in Vietnam. Without an infusion of American military power, the Saigon regime was doomed. By the summer of 1965, though Congress had not formally declared war, the United States initiated a massive bombing campaign in both South and North Vietnam, designed to destroy the power of the insurgents. As this tactic faltered, 500,000 American troops were dispatched to South Vietnam. The dimensions of such a war in this small country defy description. Over the next decade many hundreds of thousands of Vietnamese died, as did over 50,000 Americans. At the height of the air war more tons of bombs were dropped each month than had been used in all of World War II.

Asked to explain his fixation with victory in Vietnam, Johnson was alleged to have said what his predecessors must have thought: he would not be the first President "to lose a war." But the issue went beyond both LBJ's vanity and Vietnam's particular importance. The war assumed the dimensions of a contest of wills and a proxy battle between Peking and Washington. In April 1965 LBJ declared:

> Over this war—and all Asia—is another reality: the deepening shadow of Communist China. . . . the rulers of Hanoi are urged on by Peking. . . . The contest in Vietnam is part of a wider pattern of aggressive purpose.

A month later Johnson explained that Peking had targeted "not merely South Vietnam [but all] Asia" for conquest.

Through 1967 most traditional liberal institutions and politicians voiced agreement with Johnson's vision and policy. In October 1967 Vice-President Hubert Humphrey (a war supporter right through his defeat by Nixon in 1968) declared:

> The threat to world peace is militant, aggressive Asian communism, with its headquarters in Peking. . . . The aggression of North Vietnam is but the most current and immediate action of militant Asian communism.

Two years earlier he had told George McGovern that unless the U.S. "stopped the Communists in Vietnam . . . they would take all of Asia."

The *New York Times*, eventually the foremost journalistic forum of antiwar sentiment—and publisher of the *Pentagon Papers*—came late to dissent. The paper had supported editorially the French colonial war in Vietnam, and in the early 1960s had prodded the Kennedy Administration to expand the U.S. combat presence in Southeast Asia. Following Diem's death in the 1963 coup, the *Times* expressed relief that the "new Vietnamese rulers are dedicated anticommunists who reject any idea of neutralism and pledge to stand with the free world."

As with so many grandiose American statements on the importance of the war, these totally distorted what many observers knew at the time. Within the communist camp Vietnam was tied more closely to the Soviet Union than to China. Even the basis of this tie was largely Hanoi's desperate need of modern weapons to combat the Americans. The deep, often ugly, traditional dislike between Vietnamese and Chinese resurfaced almost as soon as the war in Vietnam ended. The supposedly monolithic allies quickly regrouped their armed forces along each other's borders. By February 1979 China had begun its own Vietnam War.

Oblivious to this and many deeper contradictions, America plunged headlong into the disaster of Vietnam. Between 1965 and 1968 the U.S. carried out the most intensive bombing campaign in human history and committed an army and navy of over half a million men against the guerrilla forces of one of the more economically backward nations of the earth. But technological superiority and promises of imminent victory failed to bring Washington any closer to securing Saigon against its Vietnamese opponents. Within the United States disillusionment grew as did lists of casualties and military appropriations. Soon the immense cost of the war undercut Johnson's plans for domestic economic and social reforms—the "Great Society."* The President, to use his own phrase, was forced to sacrifice "the woman I really loved" (the Great Society) to pay for "that bitch of a war on the other side of the world. . . ." As a growing number of national politicians, scholars, students, and draftees began to voice opposition to the quagmire of Vietnam, Johnson isolated himself from critics. Increasingly suspicious that the opposition to the undeclared war was disloyal if not treasonous, LBJ ordered the FBI and CIA to monitor and even harrass antiwar organizations and individuals.

As the war escalated, so did the likelihood of a direct Chinese-American confrontation in Southeast Asia. In their attacks upon North Vietnam, American planes passed perilously close to China. Several were actually shot down after intruding into Chinese air space. As both a measure of support for Vietnam and a warning signal to Washington, between 1965 and 1968 Peking sent approximately 50,000 soldiers to North Vietnam. Though not participating in ground combat, they helped operate

---

* The huge military outlays were paid by Federal borrowing, a major factor contributing to the inflation and the economic problems of the 1970s.

antiaircraft weapons and communications facilities. Without question their presence was largely intended to warn the Americans against any invasion of the North such as MacArthur had done in Korea. Washington, having learned how seriously China would react to any ground attack upon its neighbors, exercised caution. For its part, China's growing border dispute with the Soviet Union constrained any inclination Peking may have had to assist Hanoi more directly.

The bloody fighting in Vietnam's jungles enraged a growing number of Americans. Opposition to the war grew not only on college campuses but also in Congress and in the press. Repeated promises that America had turned a corner and could now see "the light at the end of the tunnel" were belied by mounting casualty lists and ever-larger draft calls. Johnson's own optimism was shattered by the Communists' Tet Offensive, launched in February 1968. American military leaders had assured the President and public that the enemy was virtually defeated, that the end was within sight. Yet, during Tet the Vietcong demonstrated remarkable strength throughout Vietnam, actually penetrating the grounds of the "impregnable" U.S. embassy in Saigon, while attacking all the major cities of the south simultaneously. The response of the Joint Chiefs was a call to send more American troops. Clearly, the policy of escalating until the enemy (be they Vietcong or Chinese Communist) left South Vietnam in peace had borne no success. The question was no longer whether one particular military plan or another might eventually succeed. American military power could never resolve the internal political struggle in Vietnam. The foreign invaders who would have to leave turned out to be the American crusaders themselves.

On March 31, 1968, President Johnson acknowledged the failure of his policy and announced his decisions both not to seek reelection and to call a limited halt to the airwar over North Vietnam. Although the war in Vietnam would actually continue for several more years (American forces did not withdraw until early 1973, and military aid was given to Saigon until May 1975), Johnson's decision not to escalate the conflict further had a tremendous impact on domestic and foreign affairs. In their mounting frustration with "LBJ's War," the American people turned away from the Democratic Party and in the November election selected Richard Nixon as President. While he had earlier been a vociferous "hawk" on the war, in 1968 Nixon campaigned on a platform of having a "secret plan to end the war." During the six years of his presidency, Nixon would lead the American nation down many unexpected paths in Asia. None would be more unpredictable than his policies toward Vietnam and China.

Selected Additional Readings

America's quarter-century involvement in Vietman is the subject of a growing literature. Hoopes, *The Devil and John Foster Dulles,* cited earlier, describes the initial involvement under Eisenhower. David Halberstam, *The Best and the Brightest,* New York: Random House, 1972, presents an extensive analysis of how the Kennedy Administration plunged into the war. President Johnson's outlook on Vietnam and China is elucidated in a revealing biography by Doris Kearns, *Lyndon Johnson and the American Dream,* New York: Harper and Row, 1974. A more theoretical discussion of policy is presented by Daniel Ellsberg, *Papers on the War,* New York: Simon & Schuster, 1972. Townsend Hoopes, *The Limits of Intervention,* New York: D. McKay Co., recounts the frustrations of Johnson's escalation policy.

For an eyewitness account of the impact of the war on Vietnam see Frances Fitzgerald, *Fire in the Lake: The Vietnamese and the Americans in Vietnam,* Boston: Little, Brown, 1972. The role of the CIA and organized crime in the Vietnam war is discussed in Alfred W. McCoy, *The Politics of Heroin in Southeast Asia,* New York: Harper & Row, 1972. The tense relationship between American forces in Vietnam and Communist China is discussed in Allen S. Whiting, *The Chinese Calculus of Deterence: India and Indochina,* Ann Arbor: University of Michigan Press, 1975.

An extremely critical overview of U.S. activities in Indochina is presented by the Committee of Concerned Asian Scholars, *The Indochina Story,* New York: Bantam, 1970; An ex-CIA agent, Frank Snepp, recounts the chaos surrounding the end of the Vietnam War in *Decent Interval,* New York: Random House, 1978.

8

The Long Journey: Sino-American Détente

In January 1969, as a new administration assumed power in Washington, few Americans still voiced enthusiasm for the war in Vietnam. Some felt the war was justified but unwinnable. Others condemned it as a senseless, immoral slaughter. Whatever the basis of their criticism, most "hawks" and "doves" agreed that the Asian policy of the United States was a shambles. Washington seemed unable either to destroy the Vietcong or to silence the growing peace movement at home. Although a succession of presidents had approved of the war to demonstrate American power and unity, the policy had proved a dismal failure.

Even while President Johnson was expanding the war after 1965, an impressive number of American opinion leaders—journalists, scholars, members of Congress—began to question the conventional wisdom which sanctioned unremitting hostility towards China and communism in Asia. At the same time, many of Chiang Kai-shek's political allies in the U.S. had grown old, disinterested and tired of the battle. In this atmosphere of war-weariness, a rethinking of old ideas became possible.

A series of hearings before Senator William Fulbright's Senate

Foreign Relations Committee in 1966 confirmed this trend. Fulbright, originally a war supporter who emerged as a leading war critic, assembled a cross-section of respected scholars and experts on Asian politics who argued that the American government had grossly misinterpreted Chinese foreign policy ever since the Second World War. They questioned Washington's depiction of the P.R.C. as a ruthless, imperialistic, communist power. To a great extent, they said, Chinese behavior was following a traditional pattern, that of reasserting leadership in East Asia, seeking friendly neighbors and demanding respect. Though Peking broadly declared its support for world revolution, and supplied limited assistance to scattered guerrilla groups, there was little real evidence to show that Communist China had tried to conquer Asia. The testimony also asserted that the North Vietnamese–Vietcong struggle to unify Vietnam had its roots primarily in nationalism, rather than in a communist plan for world domination. While several painful years would elapse before American political leaders were to accept these concepts, a new perspective had been offered by those on the fringes of influence. China, it proposed, might have just aspirations in Asia and realistic grievances against American actions. Understanding Communist China was now more crucial than ever, for in October 1964 the People's Republic had exploded its first nuclear device. By 1967 Peking had developed a hydrogen bomb and in 1970 orbited its first earth satellite.

In many ways it remains an historical irony that the American leader who reestablished a dialogue with China was Richard Nixon, a politician whose entire prepresidential career had been highlighted by unremitting opposition to revolutionary movements. Early in the 1950s, Nixon endorsed McCarthy's charge that treasonous diplomats had "lost China." In 1954, while Vice-President, he had urged Eisenhower to send American forces to Vietnam; during the crises over the offshore islands in 1955 and 1958 he was most adamant about not surrendering a foot of territory to the Chinese Communists; when debating John Kennedy in October 1960 he had declared: "Now what do the Chinese Communists want? They don't just want Quemoy and Matsu. They don't just want Formosa. They want the world."

As spokesman for the Republican Party in 1965 he criticized President Johnson for not doing enough to resist the Chinese and Vietnamese Communists. Since 1949, in effect, Nixon had continually opposed any "softening" of United States policy towards Peking.

Until he assumed the Presidency, Nixon gave little indication that his earlier opinions had changed to any great degree. In an article appearing in a 1967 issue of the influential journal *Foreign Affairs* ("Asia After Vietnam"), Nixon urged that the United States give even greater assistance to its Southeast Asian allies to contain China militarily. He reaffirmed his opposition to granting China diplomatic recognition, U.N. membership, or trade privileges. American policy, he argued, should be "to persuade China that it must change: that it cannot satisfy its imperialistic ambitions." In a significant ambiguity, however, Nixon implied that when and if China did change its behavior the U.S. might reassess its own frozen attitudes.

For better or worse the Nixon presidency put U.S. foreign policy on an irreversible course. It marked a belated acceptance of a limited role in Southeast Asia; a realization that the U.S. must live with nuclear parity with the Soviets; a diminished role for America as world policemen; and a determination to bring China into world councils.

Nixon's willingness to pursue new approaches towards China after 1969 reflected an understanding on his part that the politics of Asia were far more complicated than the United States had realized for a generation. Yet, even this realization gained slow acceptance. The failure to achieve victory in Vietnam crumbled one pillar of American policy. But it required the outbreak of virtually open warfare between the Russians and Chinese to undermine Washington's fixation on the specter of "monolithic communism." More than any other factor, the Sino-Soviet split was the force which drove the United States and China towards a new relationship.

Tension between the Chinese and Soviet communists had a long and clouded history. As far back as the 1920s, Stalin had opposed Mao's doctrines of peasant revolution. During the Second World War, Mao and Chou had frequently hinted to Americans that the CCP preferred to keep its distance from Moscow, but that Washington would force them to side more openly with Stalin if it continued to support Chiang. Not only did American leaders reject this course, but, after 1949, they also insisted that the Chinese Communists were slavish servants of the Kremlin.

The Sino-Soviet alliance proved far stormier than most Americans realized. From its inception in 1950, the Chinese harbored many grievances about Russian aid. Although Stalin had granted China several hundred million dollars' worth of credits, he insisted that China pay for the almost $1 billion worth of military equipment it desperately required during the Korean War. Stalin also insisted that the Soviet Union keep its special port, naval and railroad privileges in Manchuria. Only after the long-time Soviet leader's death in 1953 did the new Russian leadership agree to a more generous aid package and the complete abandonment of Soviet facilities in Manchuria.

From the mid-1950s on, Sino-Soviet relations continued to deteriorate. Mao believed that Moscow must not only accept the Chinese as full "partners" in the communist movement, but must also admit that the Chinese political and economic model of development was especially applicable to the "third world." Mao launched such programs as the Great Leap Forward in 1958—a mass campaign to communize agriculture and inspire rapid industrialization through revolutionary zeal—in direct opposition to the Soviet model of proper development. In 1957 Mao had given a speech in Moscow which declared "the East Wind is prevailing over the West Wind." This symbolized much more than his belief that communism was the wave of the future. In essence, Mao was saying that China's revolutionary experience would become the example for all developing nations, not the program advanced by the already industrialized and European-oriented Soviet Union.

Despite Chinese calls for a Soviet commitment to aid China and other revolutionary movements with greater economic and military assistance, the Soviet leadership refused to budge. Nikita S. Khrushchev and his fellow Russian leaders had, in fact, become more cautious as their nation achieved a more secure military and economic level. Now they advocated "peaceful coexistence" with the United States and other capitalist nations. According to the Chinese, the Russian line betrayed the long-term goals of world revolution. These political and theoretical disputes opened a widening rift between the Soviet Union and the People's Republic of China.

When China and the U.S. neared a military confrontation over the blockade of Quemoy island in 1958, the Russians showed their displeasure with Peking by pledging only half-hearted commitment to the Sino-Soviet defense treaty. Shortly thereafter, in 1959, Khrushchev gave cautious verbal support (followed by economic aid) to India, then in a protracted border dispute with China. That same year Moscow broke a promise to assist China with the development of atomic weapons. By the early 1960s it seemed as though the Soviet Union had not only drifted apart from China politically but had begun to see it as a military rival. When the long-festering Sino-Indian border dispute led to a brief war in 1962 (now generally blamed on India's refusal to reach a reasonable compromise), the Soviet Union supported the Indians with military and economic aid.

From this time forward, relations between the two communist neighbors grew ever more hostile. China's 4,500 mile border with the Soviet Union remained poorly demarked, and both nations harbored an intense historic territorial rivalry. Ever since Czarist Russian explorers had ventured across Siberia in the seventeenth century, China had been steadily losing territory to the Russians. Large tracts were acquired by the "unequal treaties" of the nineteenth century. But even the "fraternal" Soviet Union had itself made Outer Mongolia a satellite and kept imperialistic privileges in Manchuria until the mid-1950s. Once their ideological split had widened into a chasm, Moscow and Peking accused each other of planning to seize more land along their common borders. The Soviet invasion of Communist Czechoslovakia in August 1968 (which Moscow justified as its right in order to depose an increasingly independent socialist regime) terribly frightened Peking. The Soviets had demonstrated their willingness and ability to attack a former ally strayed from the fold. China's most extreme anxiety about Russian intentions seemed confirmed.

In March 1969 Chinese and Soviet armed forces clashed over one of the islands along the course of the Amur and Ussuri Rivers. By the summer of 1969, after additional local skirmishes, both nations began to shift substantial military forces into the disputed region. The Soviets brought up approximately thirty-five divisions armed with nuclear weapons and transferred bomber units from Eastern Europe. Since 1969, rumors of impending war or perhaps a Soviet nuclear strike against China have circulated periodically.*

Since the late 1960s Chinese defense policy has been aimed primarily against the USSR. Soviet "social imperialism," rather than American imperialism, came to be labeled the "#1 enemy" of peace. Chairman Mao transmitted this message to the Chinese people by instructing them to "store grain and dig tunnels deeply," as precautions against a Soviet attack or invasion.

Given China's simultaneous concern with the American presence in Vietnam, it is not difficult to imagine the terror which the Peking leadership must have felt over Soviet behavior. Peking could not fully fathom Moscow's intentions, nor the course which the new Nixon Administration might follow. Faced with hostile forces on two fronts, the Chinese might well have thought that the United States and Russia had entered an implicit alliance to surround China with their armies.

In 1969 China was just emerging from its own internal upheaval, the "Great Proletarian Cultural Revolution." Launched by Mao four years earlier, the Cultural Revolution was a mass political campaign aimed at rekindling the fervor of revolution in China. Mao and a group of "radical" supporters seemed fearful that a conservative bureaucratic elite was emerging and argued that it must be smashed before it grew too strong. Additionally the Cultural Revolution may have aimed at toppling from power Communist officials thought to be pro-Soviet in outlook.

After more than ten years' distance, both American scholars and the Chinese people themselves still differ about the purpose and accomplishments of the Cultural Revolution. Mao's supporters as well as his opponents in China acted from a variety of political and personal motives. Most American political officials

---

* In 1969, to frighten the Chinese, Soviet spokesmen circulated rumors of a possible "pre-emptive" attack against Chinese nuclear facilities. U.S. officials, who in 1963 expressed similar ideas, now stated their opposition to any such adventure. By 1979 almost one million Soviet troops faced China.

at the time tended to overlook the ambiguities of Chinese politics and the evidence of internal turmoil. President Johnson's advisors, in particular, took at face value many exaggerated statements emerging from China and held them out as proof of Peking's utter madness. Until 1969, few foreign policy experts in Washington were prepared to accept or understand China's fear of being pinned between Soviet and American power.

By the time Nixon assumed the Presidency in January 1969, however, this simple-minded outlook gave way to more serious reevaluation. Nixon and his National Security Advisor, Dr. Henry Kissinger, understood that the Sino-Soviet conflict and the reverses America had already suffered in Vietnam must radically alter the past positions of both the United States and China. Washington no longer assumed that it could impose its military and political will upon East Asia; China had lost its major economic and military ally and now stood vulnerable between the Soviet Union and the United States.

Whatever their earlier fears of Communist China, Nixon and Kissinger acknowledged that Peking faced a serious Soviet threat. In light of this fact, they reasoned, China might be willing to make concessions to Washington in order to reduce tensions and be able to marshal its limited strength against Russia. By conceding to China a greater role in Asia and the world, the United States might be able to gain increased leverage over a nervous Soviet Union. Nixon and Kissinger envisioned a "multipolar world," in which the United States, the Soviet Union, China, Japan and Western Europe would each enjoy a sphere of interest. This was an aspect of "détente," an accommodation to the fact that the powerful, established nations of the world must coexist peacefully or risk nuclear destruction. The United States had not abandoned its opposition to radical social change in general, but was willing to tolerate Soviet or Chinese domination of a defined sphere of interest. At the same time Washington hoped that it could exploit the opportunity of the Sino-Soviet split to play off Moscow and Peking against one another.

Improved contacts with China promised two immediate benefits for the U.S. The Russians might be more willing to reach certain political and arms limitations agreements with the United States to prevent a possible Sino-American alliance against themselves. Also, in order to court Washington's favor against Moscow, Peking might be willing to assist America in pressuring Hanoi to agree upon a settlement of the Vietnam War. These two considerations gave the Nixon Administration an impetus to improve relations with China soon after taking office.

During 1969, it appears, the Chinese shared Washington's perception of the various problems it faced. Mao and Chou did not suddenly fall in love with the United States, but realized that a détente with America would permit China to counter more effectively the immediate threat presented by the Soviet Union. Almost as soon as Nixon took office the Chinese began signalling Washington that they wished to improve their relations with the United States.

The decision by Nixon and Kissinger to pursue a new relationship with China faced a peculiar problem in Washington. Ever since 1949 all planning and policies regarding China were conditioned by the fact of Sino-American hostility. The policy formulating staffs of the State Department, National Security Council, CIA, Defense, Treasury, and Commerce departments had spent twenty years trying to "contain" Chinese Communism and interfere with the internal and foreign policies of the P.R.C. Dozens of military agreements, trade sanctions and propaganda machines were all arrayed against China. As China expert Michel Oksenberg (appointed to the National Security Council staff by President Carter) wrote, throughout the government "vested bureaucratic interests developed around a hostile policy towards China; no bureaucracy had an interest in improving relations with China. . . . the McCarthy era showed what could happen to an individual within those hostile structures who might argue that our national interest was not well served by all of this." In pursuit of change Nixon and Kissinger had almost no choice but to form a "cabal" against vested anti-China organs inside the U.S. government—organs Nixon himself had helped create.

The Great Turnaround

Not surprisingly, both Washington and Peking found it difficult to reverse twenty years of unremitting hostility. Continued

American participation in the Vietnam War and the feeling among Mao's more radical followers that no compromise with America was possible or justified compounded the problem. Although Nixon and Kissinger had already decided upon a gradual Vietnam withdrawal, they were unprepared to abandon Saigon suddenly and risk a domestic backlash. Their behavior might be compared to the lawman in a frontier fable: they would back out of the saloon with both guns blazing.

Hoping to leave the South Vietnamese regime with some temporary breathing space, termed "a decent interval," Nixon and Kissinger actually approved an expansion of the war against the communist forces in Southeast Asia. In March 1970 neutralist Prince Sihanouk of Cambodia was overthrown in what was probably a CIA-assisted coup. His successor, General Lon Nol, received increasing amounts of U.S. aid in an ultimately futile attempt to preserve his rule. Outraged by this reescalation of the war, Mao personally denounced America's action in Cambodia, calling upon the "people of the world" to "unite and defeat the U.S. aggressors and all their running dogs."

Washington then secretly expanded the Vietnam War into neighboring Laos in the spring of 1971, hoping to destroy communist sanctuaries there. Chou En-lai responded to this challenge by flying to Hanoi to publicly renew China's pledge of support against the United States. China, he asserted, would be the "reliable rear area," helping the revolutionary struggles of Southeast Asia against attacks by American imperialism.

In light of these events, both the hostile rhetoric and military confrontations of the past seemed unabated. Yet, important changes were taking place in the perceptions that Peking and Washington had of each other. Despite the new involvement in Cambodia and Laos, American ground troops were being gradually withdrawn from Vietnam. By May 1971 Nixon had almost halved their number from the 1968 level. Meanwhile, China witnessed the ominous buildup of Soviet conventional and nuclear forces all along its northern border. The Chinese leadership saw this as a much more immediate threat to their nation's security. American containment, it seemed, was being overshadowed by Soviet encirclement. The Chinese increasingly denounced Soviet "social imperialism" as an even greater threat than American imperialism. This new threat prompted China to begin a quiet approach toward Washington.

Soon after Nixon's election, Peking suggested publicly that "peaceful coexistence" should be pursued by America and China. Then, at a reception, a Chinese diplomat told an American that the two nations ought to resume their suspended ambassadorial discussions. (Since 1955, occasional talks, first in Geneva, then Warsaw, had been held between U.S. and Chinese ambassadors.) Although Nixon agreed, the Chinese suddenly cancelled the proposed Warsaw meeting at the last moment. Apparently, the Peking leadership was itself divided on what approach to take to the United States. The Warsaw talks, moreover, were of limited value since both parties assumed the Russians "bugged" the meetings. Then, in July 1969, the State Department announced a relaxation of the restrictions on American travel to China. Henceforth, students, scholars, doctors and scientists would be issued passports specially validated for China. Since Peking still barred most Americans—explaining that Washington's action fell short of acknowledging Peking's legitimacy—the act was largely symbolic. Nevertheless, the announcement was the first sign of an American policy change in many years.

Chinese-Soviet tensions remained a powerful catalyst for change. In March 1969, Soviet and Chinese troops fought two battles along the Ussuri River. If a wider war developed, the Chinese had a very limited ability to match Soviet strength. This fact made improved relations with Washington a vital requirement of Chinese security. By January 1970 Peking again suggested resumption of ambassadorial talks with Washington and two meetings were quickly held before the Cambodian coup of March 1970 temporarily stopped progress.

A few months later, during the summer of 1970, Peking again sent signals that it desired to resume a dialogue with the United States. Because the Warsaw talks were no longer an appropriate forum for discussion, the Chinese relied on symbolic gestures and messages carried by go-betweens, who included private Americans and leaders of nations on good terms with China. In July Peking released from prison an American Catholic bishop who had been held since 1958. In August American journalist Edgar Snow was invited for an extended visit to China. Snow's

1938 book, *Red Star Over China,* had catapulted the then little-known Mao and CCP to world fame, and he was widely known as a "favorite" American among the Chinese leaders. While in China Snow was accorded the unusual privilege of interviewing both Mao and Chou and actually stood beside Mao in reviewing the October 1 National Day parade.

Within China, the leadership itself appeared divided over how to proceed. Mao's most radical supporter and heir apparent, Defense Minister Lin Piao, seemed opposed to détente with Washington. Other officials rejected the idea that relations could be improved while the United States remained committed to the defense of Taiwan. Nevertheless, between August and September, Mao and Chou's more moderate policy prevailed. These men understood that China could not possibly deter a Soviet attack if Washington remained an active enemy. Liberating Taiwan was an issue which could be postponed for later solution.

The victory of the "moderates" cleared the path for new openings. Mao told Edgar Snow during a December 18, 1970, interview that Nixon's personal history of anticommunism should not block improved relations, that "at present the problems between China and the U.S.A. would have to be solved with Nixon. Mao would be happy to talk with him, either as a tourist or as President." In an incident of historical irony, word of Mao's startling invitation to his old enemy was presented to the American people in an article Snow published in *Life* magazine. The former vehicle for the China Lobby had now become a messenger of quite a different sort. The White House learned of Mao's remarks to Snow almost immediately after they were made.

During late 1970 Nixon and Kissinger grew increasingly frustrated by the inability of U.S. military offensives in Cambodia and Laos to "soften" up the North Vietnamese negotiating position. In a flanking move, designed in part to scare Hanoi, Nixon decided to step up the pace of his approach towards China. In late October, during a news conference, Nixon made reference to the "People's Republic of China." This marked the first time an American president had publicly used the real name of the Peking regime: implicitly it acknowledged the legal existence of that government. During the same period of time Pakistani

President Yahya and Romanian President Ceausescu served as intermediaries, carrying messages between Washington and Peking. Chou En-lai, in a conversation with a Romanian official, hinted that U.S.-P.R.C. relations might be established without a formal U.S. break with Taiwan.

President Nixon eagerly responded to and encouraged the Mao-Chou policy line. The President's address to Congress on February 25, 1971, provided a deep clue that something important was brewing. That Richard Nixon expressed the following thoughts was all the more remarkable. Nixon deplored the twenty-two years of Sino-American hostility, stating that:

> In this decade, therefore, there will be no more important challenge than that of drawing the People's Republic of China into a constructive relationship with the world community. . . . We are prepared to establish a dialogue with Peking. We cannot accept its ideological precepts or [its] hegemony over Asia. But neither do we wish to impose on China an international position that denies its legitimate national interests.

Nixon went on to reaffirm America's commitment to the defense of Taiwan and explained that he did not yet favor the admission of China to the U.N. Nevertheless, he promised:

> In the coming year I will carefully examine what further steps we might take to create broader opportunities for contacts between the Chinese and American peoples, and how we might remove needless obstacles to the realization of these opportunities. We hope for, but will not be deterred by a lack of, reciprocity. . . .

The President's words were quickly followed by a decision on March 15, 1971, to remove all remaining passport restrictions on travel by Americans to China. They would no longer be required to apply for a special stamp which China claimed insulted its sovereignty. This ended a twenty-year-old policy. The Chinese responded almost at once to this signal. An American table-tennis team, currently in Japan, was quickly issued an invitation to compete in China. The Nixon Administration quickly gave its blessing to the idea. This visit gave birth to the phrase "ping-pong diplomacy."

The team of young American athletes was accompanied by

an entourage of U.S. journalists when they arrived in China in April 1971, ending the information blockade which limited communication between the two countries since 1949. The importance which the Chinese gave to the occasion was highlighted when Premier Chou greeted the visiting team, telling the Americans that "your visit to China on invitation has opened the door to friendly contacts between the people of the two countries." On the same day Chou greeted the American athletes, Nixon announced that he was preparing to abandon the general trade embargo which had been imposed on China since the Korean War.

Nixon's initiatives toward Peking were made possible, in part, by a new mood in the United States. As informal contacts with China became more common, few Americans stood up to denounce the perfidy of dealing with "godless Red China." Most political leaders, the media and a large majority of the public seemed ready to accept a change. President Nixon, moreover, had a tremendous advantage over all his predecessors. He was the first president since 1949 who did not have to fear being attacked by politician Richard Nixon for being "soft on communism!" His anticommunist credentials were clean. The receptiveness he found both in America and among Chinese leaders encouraged Nixon to proceed with more formal contacts.

The visit of the American ping-pong team initiated a policy of "people-to-people" contacts between Americans and Chinese. Soon a number of delegations of American students, scholars and journalists were invited to China. Among the guests were several of the American diplomats and scholars (including John Service and John K. Fairbank) who had been accused of disloyalty for their accurate reporting of Chinese politics during WWII.

However useful these exchanges were, the problem of establishing formal political contact still remained. The Nixon Administration sought to breach this barrier by accepting Chou En-Lai's invitation of April to send Henry Kissinger on a secret mission to Peking. Kissinger's mission had to be kept under wraps for several reasons. No one knew what fruits it might yield. The Chinese feared provoking a Russian reaction and arousing the ire of their own radical factions. Nixon still harbored some doubts about how conservative Americans would react to his diplomatic venture. Furthermore, Washington was proceeding with his mission without any consultation with its Japanese allies.

By mid-1971 the close partnership between Japan and the U.S. which had prevailed since the Korean War had begun to show strains. Increasingly, the two nations were becoming trade rivals and finding it difficult to agree upon how to deal with China. The Nixon Administration's disdain for Tokyo was demonstrated by the manner in which the White House undertook a unilateral decision to devalue the dollar in relation to the yen. While this act would have a serious affect on the Japanese economy, Nixon publicly announced the devaluation without bothering to consult Japan. Adding insult to injury, the action was taken on the anniversary of Japan's WWII surrender, August 15, 1971. This action, when combined with the American decision to ignore its ally when dealing with China, confirmed Japan's suspicion of being a very secondary concern of American Asian policy. The President succeeded in adding another new English word to the Japanese vocabulary: "Nixon Shock."

The Kissinger Mission

Early in July, accompanied by three close aides, National Security Advisor Henry Kissinger flew from Pakistan to Peking. He arranged the trip in utmost secrecy, feigning sickness to win a few days out of the spotlight while on a foreign tour. The Kissinger-Chou conversations proved frank and useful. Chou wanted the U.S. to acknowledge Taiwan as part of China, a province whose fate should be decided by the Chinese. He expected Washington to break relations with Taiwan and end its defense commitment to the Nationalist regime. Kissinger declared that the U.S., while not willing to immediately abandon Taiwan, would be happy to establish an intermediate form of diplomatic relations with the P.R.C. U.S. military ties to Japan, Korea and the Philippines posed no problem, since Peking now preferred to see them maintained as a barrier to the Soviets. On July 10, Chou En-lai formally invited Nixon to visit China, a sign that the preliminary talks had been successful.

On July 15, 1971, Richard Nixon stunned the world by going

on television to announce that Henry Kissinger had just returned from a week-long visit to China. The initial talks had proved so productive, Nixon explained, that he would accept a Chinese invitation to visit Peking early in 1972. The American public reacted with excitement and approval to an announcement that promised to speed termination of both Sino-American hostility and the seemingly endless war in Vietnam.

Ironically, Peking appeared to have a more difficult time selling the Nixon visit than did the President. The more radical faction in China, led by Lin Piao, Mao's heir apparent, vigorously opposed the prospect of détente. Between July and September, 1971, a major power struggle erupted between the "moderates," led by Chou En-lai and supported by Mao, and the "radicals," led by Defense Minister Lin Piao. Peking has never fully explained the policy advocated by Lin, accusing him instead of personal disloyalty to Mao and the Chinese Communist Party. Undoubtedly, many other domestic issues, not just the Nixon visit, separated the moderate and radical factions in China. Whatever the case, in September Lin disappeared and was later reported killed in a plane crash. Chinese officials claimed he had attempted to assassinate Mao and seize power. After this plot failed, Lin and his followers allegedly fled in a doomed effort to reach the Soviet Union. Although we may never know how much of this story is true, the power struggle was clearly decided in favor of the moderates who had invited Nixon to China. Kissinger made a second visit to Peking in October to confirm arrangements for the President's trip.

An interesting footnote to Kissinger's October mission to Peking was his crossing paths there with former diplomat John Service, also on a visit. Apparently, one of Kissinger's aides thought it might be useful for the President's National Security Advisor to speak with Service, who during WWII had had extensive contact with Mao and Chou. When the two Americans were introduced, however, Kissinger seemed ignorant of Service's unique experiences and ended the meeting after some perfunctory remarks. His behavior suggests that even the highest American officials were still unprepared to take seriously those diplomats who had campaigned for Chinese Communist–American détente twenty-five years before Nixon and Kissinger.

The impending Chinese-American summit had an immediate impact upon world politics. Obviously, the United States could no longer actively campaign to bar China from U.N. membership. But in an effort to save a seat for Taiwan, Washington announced belated support for "two China policy." Peking, it now argued, should gain a seat on the Security Council while Taiwan should be permitted to retain a seat in the less important General Assembly. This arrangement was not at all popular with most nations and especially not to China. When a vote was taken in October, the U.N. membership finally voted to expel Taiwan completely and grant sole recognition to the People's Republic. In 1972 Japan established full diplomat relations with Peking (after having long deferred to U.S. wishes that it *not* do so) and by 1979 more than one hundred other countries had followed suit.

China's admission to the United Nations in late 1971 symbolized its formal reentry into the community of nations. The isolation of the post–Korean War period was finally ending, and now China was eager for new forms of contact. Among other things, the Chinese leadership hoped that more normal political relations with the United States, Europe and Japan would yield trade and technological benefits. Since 1949 China had either "gone it alone" economically or relied on Soviet assistance. The latter was no longer possible and in order to overcome their relative backwardness, Chinese leaders were now more willing to import foreign technology. Détente with the West and Japan would make possible more rapid modernization of the economy and increase military security—vis à vis the Soviet Union.

The Nixon Visit and its Aftermath

President Nixon's departure for China on February 17, 1972, was surrounded by a degree of pomp, circumstance and "hype" unsurpassed since Dorothy and Professor Marvel prepared to fly by balloon from Oz to Kansas. Plans for the four-day-long journey (scheduled so that the President would always be landing or taking off during prime T.V. time and would reach his distination without jet lag) were programmed precisely. The Chinese and American governments arranged for an advance team of reporters to precede the Presidential plane so that live T.V. coverage could be flashed via satellite to the United States. Though space was limited, a last minute decision included Mrs. Nixon's personal hairdresser on the roster of Air Force One.

As Nixon deplaned in Peking on February 21, the flair of meticulous public relations enhanced the real drama of the event. His enthusiastic handshake with Chou En-lai symbolically overshadowed the snub John Foster Dulles had shown Chou at the Geneva Conference. The reporters accompanying the American delegation provided the first sympathetic impressions of Chinese life seen by a mass audience in the United States. Citizens of the People's Republic, despite their very different politics and culture, appeared to be human beings, not just "blue ants" or a "yellow horde."

Once in China, the Nixon-Kissinger entourage enjoyed a crowded schedule of intense negotiations and playful sightseeing. Almost as soon as they arrived, Mao invited them to a private audience, signifying his approval for the summit meeting. This meeting consisted largely of an exchange of pleasantries and reference to broad concerns. The substantive negotiations were conducted by Chou En-lai and Chiao Kuan-hua over the following four days. Nixon alternated between jaunts to the Great Wall and intricate discussions on the many points of Sino-American conflict.

On February 27, 1972, as the week-long Presidential visit neared its end, Chinese and American leaders issued the "Shanghai Communiqué." This carefully worded document articulated the new contours of the Sino-American relationship. Both parties agreed that "countries, regardless of their social systems, should conduct their relations on the principle of respect for the sovereignty and territorial integrity of all states." Tensions would be relaxed by expanding nongovernmental "people-to-people contacts" and mutually beneficial bilateral trade. Both governments expressed the hope for the further improvement of their relationship since "the normalization of relations between the two countries is not only in the interest of the Chinese and American peoples but also contributes to the relaxation of tension in Asia and the world." (In his private comments to Chinese

Chairman Mao receives President Nixon and Henry Kissinger in Peking, February 1972.

leaders—according to those who saw the transcript—Nixon actually promised to establish full diplomatic ties with Peking and sever relations with Taiwan after the 1972 election. His subsequent Watergate problems, however, deferred such a move.)

Although the affirmative, friendly tone of the joint statement represented a real breakthrough, major issues still separated the two nations. Each side insisted upon a separate declaration concerning Taiwan. "The Chinese side reaffirmed its position: the Taiwan question is the crucial question obstructing the normalization of relations. . . . Taiwan is a province of China. . . ." Accordingly, China had a right and a duty to "liberate" Taiwan by any means it chose without outside interference. To normalize U.S.-China relations, Washington must sever its ties with Taiwan and remove its forces from the island.

The position stated by the United States appeared as something of a mirror image. It acknowledged that "Taiwan is part of China" but insisted that the U.S. would only withdraw its military forces from the island "as the tension in the area diminishes" and when the two rival regimes reached a peaceful settlement. Without some form of assurance from Peking that no invasion was planned, the U.S. would not abrogate its 1954 mutual defense treaty with Taiwan.

Of course, these contrary assertions were not new. Now, however, both governments seemed determined to proceed with Sino-American détente despite their remaining differences over Taiwan. Though the Communist leaders would not admit it openly, they were prepared to defer the question of Taiwan to the future. Nixon and Kissinger seemed convinced that with the end of the Vietnam war approaching, the reduction of tensions in East Asia would permit a gradual U.S. military disengagement from Taiwan. Since China lacked the naval and air power required for an invasion of the island, the military security of Taiwan seemed assured for the foreseeable future regardless of Peking's claims.

In May 1973, following several more Kissinger trips to China, the two nations agreed to establish "liaison offices" in their respective capitals. These unofficial embassies served as an important forum for ongoing political talks. In the aftermath of the Nixon visit other changes occurred in the Sino-American relationship. Initially, trade between the two nations soared. Mostly this consisted of Chinese purchases of American cereal grains. China had little besides handicrafts to export to the United States. Although China's purchases from the U.S. rose to $900 million in 1974, the total soon declined. When it became clear that Washington would not quickly establish full diplomatic relations with Peking, the Chinese shifted their purchase of grain to other exporting nations.

The creation of liaison offices in Peking and Washington in May 1973 proved to be a plateau in the new Sino-American relationship. Following this, both countries seemed uncertain of their future course. Yet, much had already been accomplished. Peking had insured that Moscow would think very hard before undertaking any military moves against China, while Washington had established a framework for the post-Vietnam era in East Asia. The dialogue with China, and that nation's growing trade, cultural and political contacts with the West and Japan, were actually far better ways to stabilize Asia than the maintenance of hostile regimes on China's borders. Nevertheless, domestic political turmoil on both sides of the Pacific slowed the pace of détente.

President Nixon's mounting involvement in the Watergate scandal by the spring of 1973 prevented any dramatic moves toward closer relations. Unwilling to risk antagonizing his conservative supporters who maintained a fondness for Taiwan, Nixon broke a tacit promise to the Chinese to establish formal diplomatic relations once he was reelected. Gerald Ford's presidency, from August 1974 to January 1977, was largely a caretaker administration. When the accidental president did travel to Peking in December 1975, little of the Nixon-visit drama was in the air. Kissinger and Ford were not prepared to move forward toward a full diplomatic relationship with China, fearing such a move would jeopardize sensitive negotiations with the Russians on arms limitations.

The new relationship between Peking and Washington had an indirect effect upon ending the war in Vietnam. Originally, of course, American leaders had justified intervention in Southeast Asia as a struggle to "contain" Chinese expansion. Now, given the more tolerant view of China, and considering China's preoccupation with the "Soviet threat," there seemed little danger of armed Chinese expansion in Asia. In fact, Washington now hoped that Chinese power would help to offset Soviet influence in Asia and elsewhere. These factors totally undercut America's position in Vietnam, while the war itself only inhibited closer Sino-American relations.

Terminating American involvement in Vietnam, however, proved a very difficult task for the Nixon Administration. For one thing, détente with China and the U.S.S.R. marked a policy of accommodating the realities of Chinese and Soviet power. It did not signify the end of American opposition to regional revolutionary movements, or termination of aid to anticommunist regimes. During the early 1970s Nixon and Kissinger engineered a successful coup against the Allende regime in Chile and stepped up military aid to Iran and South Vietnam. Even as American forces were being withdrawn from Southeast Asia, Washington continued to believe that its policy of "Vietnamization" would allow the noncommunist forces in South Vietnam to hang on for a "decent interval."

During the summer and autumn of 1972 (as Nixon prepared to meet the challenge of antiwar candidate George McGovern), U.S. and North Vietnamese negotiators devised a compromise formula to end stalemated peace talks. The U.S. declared a willingness to pull out all remaining ground and air forces from South Vietnam within four months in exchange for an in-place cease-fire (leaving North Vietnamese and Vietcong troops in control of large parts of the south—something Nixon had pledged never to do) and the return of all U.S. POWs. Hanoi dropped its insistence that the U.S. depose the Thieu regime in Saigon as a prelude to a cease-fire. Instead, it would settle for an in-place truce, the rapid departure of all American forces and a promise that some form of coalition political structure soon be created in the south.

Although Nixon announced a virtual peace agreement just before the 1972 presidential elections, he backpeddled shortly after his overwhelming electoral victory. More time was needed to beef up Saigon's forces and demonstrate to Hanoi that they ought not to overrun the south immediately after the American withdrawal. During December 1972 Nixon ordered the U.S. Air Force to conduct a massive bombing campaign against the North Vietnamese capital. The "Christmas Bombing" coincided with a huge airlift of military equipment to Saigon. The message contained in these acts was twofold: Hanoi was shown how Washington might react to any early offensive against the south; the Thieu regime in Saigon was shown that it could afford to accept the cease-fire agreements since it had acquired a vast new stockpile of arms.

The final peace agreement signed in Paris on January 13, 1973, proved to be virtually the same agreement both sides had approved in October. The few changes actually called for a more rapid U.S. departure from the south. Even more incredible were the contents of a secret letter sent by Nixon to Hanoi. In it he promised North Vietnam almost $5 billion of postwar economic aid, with no strings attached! (Nixon and Kissinger denied this until Hanoi later made the letter public.)

In practice, the Paris Peace Agreement proved an impossible document. In the hours before it went into affect both communist and anticommunist forces went on an offensive to seize new territory. Departing U.S. forces transferred title to a vast amount of military equipment, violating a pledge that the U.S. would only replace old weapons, not give Saigon additional arms. Furthermore, several thousand American military personnel were quickly reassigned as "civilian advisors" to the Saigon army, thus remaining in Vietnam.

After discounting all the inflated rhetoric, this "Peace with Honor," as Nixon referred to it, represented little more than an American withdrawal. All parties understood that the rival Vietnamese factions would soon resume their battle for national unification. Nixon's hope, it seems, was that a huge infusion of military aid to Saigon, combined with a continuing threat against the North, would prevent the collapse of the South Vietnamese regime for a "decent interval." By then, perhaps, no one would blame the disaster on him.*

A brief interlude of scaled-down fighting following the American withdrawal as both sides braced themselves for a final confrontation. Early in 1975 Vietcong and North Vietnamese forces launched an offensive which tore apart the Saigon army. American-trained and -equipped forces fled the battlefield, often dropping their weapons (guns, planes, tanks) for the enemy to capture. Neither Washington nor American representatives in Vietnam would accept the debacle about to engulf them. Little preparation for an orderly evacuation was permitted. When the end came late in April 1975, thousands of hysterical Americans and Vietnamese clawed their way to the roof of the embassy in Saigon to be rescued by helicopters as the city fell. The U.S. left Vietnam with as little grace and honor as it came with.

Fortunately, despite the gruesome spectacle of Saigon's fall, America experienced no repeat of the "Who Lost China" campaign. Americans had tried to do in Vietnam what they had decided against doing in China in the late 1940s. Vietnam, most people seemed finally to realize, was not ours to lose. Military and diplomatic officials did not panic and scurry about to shore up a new Asian anticommunist alliance. In fact, by June 1977,

---

* Nixon's memoirs, published in May 1978, stated this. The disgraced ex-President claimed he had won a "peace with honor" but that congressional restrictions on any military reinvolvement in Vietnam after 1973 "lost the war."

the moribund SEATO alliance was allowed to pass out of existence with almost no publicity. The formal "containment" of China had ended.

Selected Additional Readings

Sino-Soviet hostility is analyzed in O. Edmund Clubb, *China and Russia The Great Game*, New York: Columbia University Press, 1971; John Gittings, *The World and China, 1922–1972*, New York: Harper and Row, 1974.

Contemporary East Asian international relations are discussed in A. Doak Barnett, *China and the Major Powers in East Asia*, Washington, D.C.: The Brookings Institution, 1977.

A scathing critique of the Nixon Administration's foreign policy, as well as an inside account of the trip to China, is presented by Tad Szulc, *The Illusion of Peace: Foreign Policy in the Nixon Years*, New York: Viking Press, 1978.

9
The Unfinished Agenda

The end of the war in Vietnam coincided with a series of major political changes inside China. Since the late 1930s the top leadership of the Chinese Communist Party had been drawn from a relatively small circle of long-lived individuals, headed by Chairman Mao Tse-tung. As old age took its toll, senior officials began to drop from power. The process accelerated during 1976 when Prime Minister Chou En-lai and then Chairman Mao died. (Chiang Kai-shek, a leader of the same generation, died in Taiwan in 1975.) In many ways these two leaders had represented competing factions among the Chinese Communists. Chou, who headed the administrative arm of the government, emphasized planning, order and expertise as the key to progress. Mao, always more of a visionary leader, had since the late 1950s championed grand ideological campaigns and internal political struggle as the best way to mobilize China and rejuvenate its revolution. The illness and death of these two figures provoked a conflict over the succession and the future direction of Chinese policy.

For many years the CCP had been rent by a schism pitting "moderates" and "radicals" against one another. These terms are inexact at best and often difficult to apply. Often the same individual adopted a radical stand on one issue, and a moderate stand on others. Mao is a case in point, sometimes advocating precise, cautious planning and at other times calling for "romantic" mass action to triumph over material obstacles. In general, moderates tended to favor more orderly, planned economic development. They stressed the importance of higher education, of rapid industrial growth and modernization of China's essentially backward economy over the virtues of relying on a rigid formula of egalitarianism and national self-reliance. Chou En-lai and his disciple, Teng Hsiao-p'ing, encouraged the importation of advanced technology from abroad and the use of foreign ideas to achieve the goal of "comprehensive modernization" by the year 2000.

Radicals comprised a more diverse group which stressed the primacy of ideological purity over economic performance. China, they believed, should avoid reliance on foreign technology, methods and ideas even if this slowed the pace of economic growth. Mao, often a supporter of revolutionary purity, adroitly juggled the two factions around him. It remains unclear how moderates and radicals differed (if they did so at all) on questions of relations with the United States.

During the Cultural Revolution (1965–68) Mao's wife, Chiang Ch'ing, emerged from obscurity to become a leading exponent of radical ideas. She devoted much effort to recasting all Chinese arts, culture and opera in a rigid political mold. She and three other radicals formed a powerful clique (later called "The Gang of Four") which allegedly attempted to gain total control of government policy.

Opposed to them was Chinese Prime Minister (Premier) Chou En-lai. Already suffering from a fatal cancer, Chou sought to arrange a moderate "line of succession" to himself during the 1970s by rehabilitating officials who had earlier been disgraced for being too moderate. Chief among these was Teng Hsiao-p'ing, who was restored to power by Chou in 1973 after having been purged as a "capitalist roader" during the tumultuous Cultural Revolution. Chou's death in January 1976, however, removed Teng's strongest patron. Mao, apparently, still distrusted the moderate Teng and nominated as premier the relatively unknown Hua Kuo-feng to succeed Chou as the individual in control of the government apparatus and administration of the country.

By April 1976 an increasingly feeble Mao (or the radicals surrounding him) once again drove Teng from office. The complex power rivalries increased after September 9, 1976, when Mao died at the age of eighty-three. Just one month later, on October 6, the Chinese press announced that the "Gang of Four"—Mao's widow Chiang Ch'ing, Deputy Premier Chang Ch'un-ch'iao, second-ranked CCP leader Wang Hung-wen, and Party propagandist Yao Wen-yuan—had tried to seize power. These radical leaders had all risen to prominence in the wake of Mao's Cultural Revolution in the 1960s.

Following the arrest and disgrace of the Gang of Four, a group of moderate leaders emerged to dominate Chinese politics. Hua Kuo-feng climaxed a meteoric rise by being named to replace Mao as Chairman of the Communist Party. In this position he could establish the overall goals of military, political and economic policy. In the summer of 1977 the twice-purged Teng Hsiao-p'ing was restored to the post of Vice-Premier from which he could direct the campaign to speed China's economic modernization. The new leadership, without formally rejecting Mao's radical programs of the period since the late 1950s, seemed determined to push pragmatic economic policies, restored to power many officials disgraced during the Cultural Revolution, reopened colleges and universities, and expanded trade and cultural contacts with the outside world. Early in 1978, for example, Peking concluded a major long-term trade agreement with Japan and additional trade deals (some of which involved the purchase of weapons) with the countries of Western Europe. The Chinese wished to accelerate their economic development by importing technology to be paid for by the export of raw materials, such as oil and minerals.*

During 1978 the Chinese leadership gave evidence of other major openings to the outside world. In August 1978 China

---

* The discovery of substantial oil reserves makes China a major potential energy exporter. With foreign technical assistance, oil could be sold to Japan, for instance, to pay for vital imports. By 1978 China already ranked as the tenth largest oil producer in the world.

finally concluded a friendship pact with Japan. The Treaty, under discussion ever since the two nations normalized relations in 1972, proposes a further increase in trade and cultural relations. China is increasingly turning towards Japan to acquire the investments and technological know-how needed to achieve its goal of industrial modernization. In line with this policy, CCP Chairman Hua Kuo-feng travelled to Eastern Europe in the autumn of 1978, visiting the independent communist states of Romania and Yugoslavia.

In a sentimental gesture toward their American friends, the Chinese in May 1978, invited the surviving members of the original Dixie Mission and their families to revisit Yenan. Speeches and toasts celebrated the earlier, abortive effort to secure better relations between the Chinese Communists and the United States. In discussing the prospects for the future, a Chinese spokesman noted that although Peking had shown patience in waiting for Washington to fulfill its pledge to establish normal diplomatic relations with the P.R.C., Peking "could not wait forever."

The new leadership in Peking remained extremely wary of Soviet intentions in Asia. A small border incident in May 1978 led China to claim again that Russian aggressiveness made war virtually certain. In order to shore up its relations in Asia—and prevent any Russian effort to contain China—Peking has striven to improve contacts with the noncommunist states of the region. Not only have the Chinese looked to expand trade with Japan, but they have also sent friendly envoys to consult with many former members of the defunct SEATO alliance. The "Association of Southeast Asian Nations" (ASEAN), which includes among its members Thailand, Singapore, Malaysia and the Philippines, has been courted by China. Ironically, Vietnam (which China considers "pro-Soviet") has had a difficult time getting along with its neighbor since the end of the war in Indochina.

During 1978 relations between Vietnam and China and Vietnam and Cambodia deteriorated drastically. Tens of thousands of ethnic Chinese fled Vietnam (into China) charging racial persecution. Sporadic shooting incidents erupted along the two nations' borders. Similarly, Communist Vietnam and Cambodia engaged in bloody fighting along their disputed borders, culminating in a Vietnamese conquest in January 1979. Obviously, the myth of monolithic communism could not account for the bitter ethnic and territorial rivalries of the countries of southeast Asia, many of which could be traced back for centuries.

No one could be certain how China's political evolution would affect the future of Sino-American relations. Superficially, it seemed advantageous to America to deal with the Chinese moderates who maintained a very wary attitude towards Moscow. The continued Sino-Soviet split reduced the ability of both Moscow and Peking to challenge American interests. In addition, many Americans believed, a Chinese leadership committed to economic modernization and increased foreign cultural contacts would favor stability in Asia and be more receptive to foreign trade. On the other hand, foreign observers realized that the course of China's internal politics had changed so drastically and rapidly that long-term predictions were unreliable at best. Moreover, if Russia and China actually went to war, the results would likely prove disastrous to the entire world.

Since the establishment of Chinese and American liaison offices in 1973, Washington showed reluctance to move toward full diplomatic relations. Under President Gerald Ford the pace of normalization slowed. During the first two years of the Carter Administration, movement virtually ceased. Though nearly all foreign policy experts, regardless of party, endorsed the principle of full Sino-American diplomatic relations, they disagreed over how the tie should be achieved. The key blockage remained the unresolved status of Taiwan.

Still recognized by the United States as an ally, the "Republic of China" (Taiwan) lies 100 miles off the coast of the mainland. Its authoritarian government, led since 1975 by Chiang Kai-shek's son, Chiang Ching-kuo, rules 18 million people. By Asian standards it is a relatively prosperous society, enjoying extensive trade with the United States and Japan, among others. Foreign investments account for a substantial measure of the island's prosperity. Since the Korean War the United States had pledged itself to defend Taiwan against attack from the mainland and maintained a small military contingent on the island. The 1954 treaty formalized the U.S. defense commitment. Taiwan's own military strength, most observers agreed, was sufficient to deter any invasion for the present. America's shield, then, was more symbolic than real.

Ever since the Korean War, Peking insisted that the United States fully disengage its military forces from Taiwan and allow the island to be "liberated" and reunited with the mainland. Given Taiwan's strength and Peking's limited amphibious military power, a successful invasion was unlikely. Nevertheless, Peking insisted that Washington break relations with Taiwan and abrogate its defense agreement before relations with the People's Republic could be normalized. With equal stubbornness, Presidents Ford and Carter continued to insist that America could not abrogate the defense treaty until Peking gave assurances it would not invade Taiwan.

When faced with this same impasse in 1972, the Japanese solved the dilemma handily. Tokyo broke relations with Taiwan and recognized Peking. At the same time Japan remained deeply involved in trade and investment with Taiwan through informal ties. A Japanese "private" trade mission continued to function on the island as an informal embassy handling both political and economic affairs. Chinese officials sometimes suggested that it would be acceptable to them if Washington followed Tokyo's lead. But America, unlike Japan, had a formal defense treaty with Taiwan. Presidents Nixon, Ford and Carter all felt unable to abandon Taiwan militarily in the process of normalizing Sino-American relations. To abrogate the treaty without a pledge from Peking to refrain from violence might shake the faith which Japan, South Korea and the Philippines had in U.S. defense commitments.

The Politics of Normalization

President Carter's reluctance to move towards normalizing relations with China after 1976 reflected a general ambivalence in U.S. politics. After Nixon's bold action of 1972 removed the harsh edge of Sino-American hostility, few politicians seemed sure how far or fast to proceed with the process. Nixon himself, when overwhelmed by Watergate, broke his secret pledge to sever ties with Taiwan. President Ford feared losing support for a SALT agreement with the Russians if he solidified ties with China. During his first two years in office Carter, too, found it expedient to delay normalization. Faced with a conservative backlash to the Panama Canal Treaty and SALT negotiations, Carter shied away from any move that might further antagonize conservative senators who remained fond of Taiwan.

Nevertheless, during 1978 a rapid chain of events involving China pushed the Carter Administration towards positive action. Under the joint direction of Chairman Hua Kuo-feng and Vice-Premier Teng Hsiao-p'ing (a disciple of Chou En-lai) China began a bold approach to modernization and increased foreign contacts. Teng emerged as the pivotal leader promoting the "four modernizations"—industry, agriculture, science, and defense. The outspoken Vice-Premier publicly admonished his countrymen for having lost a decade of progress during Chairman Mao's declining years. By blaming Mao's old age and his alleged manipulation by Lin Piao and the "Gang of Four," Teng finessed the issue of criticizing the previously infallible leader. Teng argued that Mao's belief in egalitarianism and economic self-reliance had been distorted so as to prevent China from accepting useful foreign ideas and objects. To become truly great required a modern economy and this meant the acquisition of foreign technology, capital, and training. China could not "go it alone" as Mao hoped. This new awareness meant forging new ties with Europe, Japan, and the United States.

During 1978 Teng and his supporters moved China along this road faster than foreigners believed possible. (Already in his mid-70's, the Vice-Premier obviously hoped to lock China into this policy before his own departure from power.) Peking began to send thousands of Chinese students abroad, including to the U.S., for advanced scientific and technical training. As with the earlier generations of students sent abroad, this group would be affected in profound ways by their exposure to foreign cultures. Similarly, China agreed to permit a growing number of foreign students, scholars, and tourists to come into the country.

China's major economic concern remains the acquisition of advanced industrial technology. It is determined to avoid a trade relationship which makes it the dumping ground for consumer goods. Instead, China plans to trade its oil, coal, and other

raw materials for oil-drilling and mining technology, steel mills,
fertilizer factories, computers, nuclear reactors, and certain defense equipment. Major deals have already been made with
France, Great Britain, West Germany, Japan, and the United
States. In another major departure from orthodox Maoist theory,
the P.R.C. has decided to speed development by inviting foreign
investors to begin joint business ventures inside China, the first
such opportunity since the revolution. While Japan has so far
profited most from these developments, during 1978 U.S.-China
trade doubled to about $1 billion. Economists estimate that this
two-way trade may reach $20 billion annually by 1985.

Economic statistics also bear directly on the political future
of Asia. In essence, China's opening to Japan and the West is a
commitment to a longterm relationship based on maintaining
stability. When Teng Hsiao-p'ing visited Tokyo in October 1978,
he affirmed China's new view of Asian politics. While signing the
earlier negotiated China-Japan Friendship Treaty, Teng made
a great show of visiting Emperor Hirohito. For decades the CCP
had castigated the Emperor as a symbol of imperialism and a
virtual war criminal. Now, embracing the traditional symbol of
the Japanese nation, the Chinese leader demonstrated Peking's
acceptance of the status quo in East Asia. By signing the pact
with Japan, China also effectively endorsed the U.S.-Japanese
military alliance and Japan's economic-security interests in South
Korea and Taiwan.*

These new external ties and visits abroad by Teng and Hua
coincided with a marked trend towards internal liberalization.
The rigid standards previously imposed on schools, culture, and
public expression were relaxed. Many artists, educators, scientists, and politicians disgraced during the Cultural Revolution
of the late 1960s reemerged to fill former posts. Universities
reopened, admitting students by competitive examination. In November and December, 1978, numerous public meetings, observed by foreign reporters, called for more "democratic" participation in political decisions and criticized past violations of

---

* In a talk with American congressmen in Peking in January 1979, Teng
specifically encouraged the U.S. and Japan to augment their military forces
in the Pacific as a barrier to "Soviet hegemony."

individual rights. These spontaneous developments gained some support from the official Chinese press and leadership.

Still, it would be foolish to interpret these signs as evidence that China is likely to become a western-style pluralist democracy. The roots of authoritarian politics and social conformity are too deeply embedded in Chinese culture and history for any such change to be likely in the near future. What these new developments do indicate—and what a broad cross section of Americans have begun to realize—is that diversity and rivalry do not necessarily mean hostility. Though a radically different society than our own, China poses little threat to our own values and security. In fact, the more involved with China the U.S. becomes, the more likely both societies will discover valuable aspects of the other.

The final decision to normalize U.S.-China relations reflected a complex political calculus. The series of startling developments inside China suggested to American leaders that China could be counted on to play a positive, active role in Asia. China's rush to acquire foreign technology also rekindled dreams of an important market. The absence of normal relations—a legal prerequisite for favorable loans, tariff, and trade arrangements—threatened American corporations with a loss of business to Japan and Western Europe.

China's continued hostility to the Soviet Union and support of efforts to limit Soviet power prompted some strategists—such as National Security Advisor Zbigniew Brzezinski—to talk of "playing the China card." By this Brzezinski apparently meant using closer U.S.-China tries as a way to contain the Soviet Union. Such reasoning is extremely dangerous, for rather than inhibiting Soviet behavior, the prospect of a Sino-American alliance might seem a provocation to the Kremlin. Moscow has, in fact, warned the British against selling warplanes to China.

Late in 1978, after assessing these factors, President Carter decided to act. The mid-term congressional elections had passed, reducing any danger that opposition to a new initiative might hurt the Democratic Party at the polls in November. Moreover, a long series of discussions conducted in China (by Leonard Woodcock, head of the Liaison Office, James Schlesinger, and

Zbigniew Brzezinski) and in Washington (with the head of the
Chinese Liaison Office, Chai Tse-min) had come close to re-
solving the problem posed by Taiwan. The Chinese no longer
called for "liberation" of the island by any means. Instead, Teng
spoke of reunification some time in the future.

Intensive discussions early in December produced a final
breakthrough. On the evening of December 15, 1978, in an address to the American people, President Carter announced that
the U.S. and the People's Republic of China "have agreed to
recognize each other and to establish diplomatic relations as of
January 1, 1979." Washington acknowledged Peking as the sole
legal capital of China. Nevertheless, Carter explained, the U.S.
would maintain "cultural, commercial and other unofficial relations with the people of Taiwan" through nongovernmental
organs. This followed the Japanese model of maintaining an unofficial embassy, to be called an "American Institute." Speaking
in a relaxed manner, the President referred to this decision as an
opportunity to resume the "long history of friendship" between
the Chinese and American peoples. Accepting political reality,
Carter declared, would strengthen world peace.

Both China and the U.S. had, in fact, faced a number of
realities. Peking significantly modified its previous conditions
regarding normalization. The American defense treaty with Taiwan would remain in effect for one year after normalization. In
a unilateral statement the U.S. asserted that it expected the
Taiwan issue to be "settled peacefully by the Chinese themselves" while Americans would continue private economic involvement on the island. Perhaps most importantly, even after
the termination of the defense treaty in 1979, the U.S. would
continue to sell weapons to Taiwan. This would insure the island's economic and military security for the immediate future,
at least. At an unprecedented news conference before foreign
journalists in Peking, Hua Kuo-feng explained that while the
P.R.C. did not approve of the sales, the American policy would
not stand in the way of full relations. In other words, Peking
implicitly accepted the maintenance of a special relationship
between the U.S. and Taiwan. To celebrate this achievement,
Teng Hsiao-p'ing would come to the U.S. on January 29, 1979.
In a typical quip, the first Chinese Communist leader to visit

"Welcome to Peking." (Tony Auth, *The Philadelphia Inquirer*)

Washington since 1949 declared he "wanted to visit America before going to see Marx."

Public reaction to this stunning reversal of policy was strangely muted. The press did not thunder its disapproval. No organized China lobby denounced Carter as a traitor. Characteristically, ultra-conservatives like Arizona Senator Barry Goldwater condemned the decision as a "cowardly act" that "stabs in the back the nation of Taiwan." He and a group of senators introduced a suit in federal court to challenge the President's authority to terminate the defense treaty without Senate approval. (The Constitution is vague on this point. Several senators who supported the suit actually approved of normalization but felt Carter should have consulted the Senate.) Public opinion polls reflected no great intensity of feeling on either side of the issue. The Republican Party, for its part, had only slim grounds on which to condemn Carter since Presidents Nixon and Ford had shared the same goal.

Within days of the Carter announcement two events occurred which, while largely symbolic, overshadowed much criticism.

Two of the most highly visible symbols of "American life" sanctified relations with China. First, the Coca-Cola company announced that as of January 1979 it, too, was going to China. Soon, the people of Shanghai would be drinking the "Real Thing," the first American consumer product to hit the China market since 1949. That same week *Time* magazine, once the KMT's leading mouthpiece in American journalism, placed the feisty Teng Hsiao-p'ing on its cover as "Man of the Year." He was the first Chinese so honored since Chiang Kai-shek—forty years before!

On January 28, 1979, Chinese Vice-Premier Teng Hsiao-p'ing began a nine-day tour of the United States. His initial public statements hailed the restoration of normal relations and denounced the threat of Soviet "hegemonism." While the Carter Administration declined to endorse Chinese attacks upon Moscow, President Carter hailed the "new and irreversible course" in Chinese-American relations. Both leaders quickly signed agreements to expand scientific and cultural exchanges. During Teng's ensuing cross-country tour, audiences back in China were treated to a virtually nonstop television documentary on the material accomplishments of American life. This proved to be one of the first "objective" glimpses of our society that ordinary Chinese have had since 1949.

After Teng's departure the Senate continued to wrestle with the language of legislation that would replace the American embassy on Taiwan with the unofficial "American Institute." While an overwhelming majority favored a new relationship with China, many Senators believed the United States had an obligation to deter the P.R.C. from attacking Taiwan. With tacit approval from President Carter, the Senate Foreign Relations Committee planned to attach a statement to the bill, creating the American Institute and declaring that any military assault on Taiwan would be a matter of "grave concern to the United States" and might lead to "appropriate" countermeasures. The Senate then proceeded to confirm the appointment of Leonard Woodcock as the first ambassador to the People's Republic of China.

As a new era of United States–China relations dawned on

March 1, 1979, peace in Asia was threatened by the two-week-old Chinese invasion of Vietnam. Tensions between these rivals followed a pattern of more than one thousand years. More recent Vietnamese actions in Cambodia, and Hanoi's friendship pact with the Soviet Union had outraged China. Yet, at least one hopeful sign emerged from the new conflict. Setting forth Washington's low-key response, President Carter stated frankly that the United States would do nothing more than urge all parties to cease fighting. America would no longer be the "policeman of Asia."

The normalization of U.S.-China relations and the growing ties between the P.R.C. and Japan meant that for the first time in the twentieth century the U.S. was on good terms with both the two major powers of East Asia. The territorial, economic, and political rivalries among these nations, which had led America into three wars in Asia since 1941, seemed largely solved. Each of the powers appeared to have accepted the value of coexistence without domination. Dangers persist, of course. Sino-Soviet hostility has already flowed into Southeast Asia where China and the U.S.S.R. each back rival client states. Japanese-Soviet relations remain tense. A divided Korea and disputed claims to off-shore oil fields on the Asian continental shelf could easily spark a military conflict. Nevertheless, in terms of its own interests, the United States may finally have achieved by peaceful means the balance for which it has searched for a century.

Selected Additional Readings

On China's future world role and possible developments in U.S.-China relations see Allen S. Whiting and Robert F. Dernberger, *China's Future: Foreign Policy and Economic Development*, New York: McGraw-Hill, 1977; Allen S. Whiting, *China and the United States: What Next*, New York: Foreign Policy Assoc., 1976; Michael Oksenberg and Robert Oxnam, *China and America: Past and Future*, New York: Foreign Policy Association, 1977.

China's future as an oil exporter, and its political ramifications, are discussed in Selig S. Harrison, *China, Oil and Asia: Trouble Ahead?* New York: Columbia University Press, 1977.

Drew Middleton analyzes the Sino-Soviet military confrontation in *The Duel of the Giants: China and Russia in Asia*, New York: Scribners, 1978.

For a discussion of Taiwan see Ralph Clough, *Island China*, Cambridge, Mass.: Harvard University Press, 1978.

Index